Get Set for English L

Titles in the GET SET FOR UNIVERSITY *series:*

Get Set for American Studies
ISBN 0 7486 1692 6

Get Set for English Language
ISBN 0 7486 1544 X

Get Set for English Literature
ISBN 0 7486 1537 7

Get Set for Geography
ISBN 0 7486 1693 4

Get Set for Linguistics
ISBN 0 7486 1694 2

Get Set for Media Studies
ISBN 0 7486 1695 0

Get Set for Philosophy
ISBN 0 7486 1657 8

Get Set for Politics
ISBN 0 7486 1545 8

Get Set for Study in the UK
ISBN 0 7486 1810 4

Get Set for English Literature

David Amigoni and Julie Sanders

Edinburgh University Press

© David Amigoni and Julie Sanders, 2003

Edinburgh University Press Ltd
22 George Square, Edinburgh

Typeset in Sabon
by Hewer Text Ltd, Edinburgh, and
printed and bound in Finland by
WS Bookwell

A CIP record for this book is
available from the British Library

ISBN 0 7486 1537 7 (paperback)

CONTENTS

Introduction   vi

PART I: STUDYING ENGLISH LITERATURE

1 What is English literature?   3
2 Why study English literature?   11
3 What forms can the study of English literature take?   20
4 The place of 'theory' in English literature programmes   47

PART II: STUDY SKILLS IN ENGLISH LITERATURE

5 Reading   67
6 Getting the most from lectures   75
7 How to use a tutorial or teaching session   80
8 Time management   92
9 Assessment   95
10 Research and writing skills   103
11 Revising for and taking examinations   125

Bibliography and further reading   132
Index   137

INTRODUCTION

'Getting Set for University Life' can mean, in the first instance, seeing to some very practical and material requirements: sorting out accommodation; mastering the local public-transport system; perhaps buying a kettle, computer and duvet for your room or lodgings; opening up a bank account; sorting out the logistics of a student loan; learning how to work the halls of residence's washing machines and how to whip up a mean spaghetti bolognese. But, sooner or later, the reality of your course requirements – in your case those of an English literature degree – hits home and, as well as all these everyday needs to answer, you will also have to determine the specific learning and studying skills demanded by the programme of study you have elected to follow. The purpose of this book is to prepare you as fully as possible for those demands. We suggest that it is best read, initially, in advance of arriving at your chosen institution, perhaps over the summer before you commence full-time or part-time studies, and then read once more alongside the Induction and Introductory sessions your university or college will no doubt offer you in those early weeks of undergraduate life. It may also prove a comforting presence on the bookshelf in your aforementioned room at home, in halls or in lodgings – where, by now, it is hoped the duvet cover and kettle will have been joined by the apparatus of study; invariably, for the literature student, books, books, and more books – to be taken down and consulted when specific issues such as time management or preparing for examinations emerge as more pressing concerns.

As its title suggests, this volume is subject-specific in its concerns; its primary aim is to prepare you for the study of English literature at university. This does not mean that some of its more general advice, particularly about skills, is inap-

plicable or irrelevant to other areas of your degree programme. Many of you, after all, will be studying joint or dual
honours programmes, where English literature is one element
of your study but not the sole focus discipline; others may be
pursuing supplementary, subsidiary or linked modules or
courses. On all of these kinds of programmes, some of the
general skills advice offered here may well prove helpful. But it
remains our essential task to help you navigate the choppy
waters of a literature programme. Our objectives are to highlight the diverse and rich ways in which you might encounter
the texts and questions your courses will invariably raise, and
to suggest some forms of best practice in areas such as
completing required assessments or preparing for the learning
situations in which you will find yourself. Our advice should
therefore be read alongside more general texts on university
life and the specific publications offered by your institution of
choice, such as prospectuses, departmental, school or faculty
handbooks, and institutional and departmental websites. It is
intended to supplement and complement the Induction sessions your own departments will offer.

We should stress from the outset that this book is not a
series of passnotes for an English degree, nor is it a detailed
introduction to the complex history of literature as a subject or
the related area of literary theory. Similarly, while it will offer
skills-based advice on writing an assessed essay or researching
a topic for a presentation, it does so in the knowledge that
there are several books currently available that treat with these
issues at length and in detail, in a way that we cannot hope to
achieve here. We have offered a list of these works for your
attention and subsequent exploration under the heading of
'Further reading' towards the end of this volume. While we
will in passing offer descriptions of why literature exists as a
discipline and what the subject might do for you as an
individual, both now and in the future, this is not a history
of the subject. What this book represents is an attempt to
prepare you for what things might look like or feel like when
you arrive at university or college to study English literature. It
is an attempt to describe the precise shape and form that your

experiences might take, from teaching methods to timetables, from lecture halls and pigeonholes, to the experience of studying itself.

As an extension of this, you will also encounter throughout the volume a varied lexicon of terms and phrases you wish to familiarise yourself with once at university. We have tried to offer clear definitions for these terms when we deploy them. Once again, this is not intended to be a comprehensive catalogue of terminology and vocabulary that you might need on a literature degree: to achieve this would require a volume in itself dedicated to the topic. Our hope is rather to familiarise you with a range of practical terms, and to render them less daunting or alien, in order to help you with that aforementioned navigation of your university degree course. Some of these terms may already be familiar from previous contexts – such as 'seminar' or 'tutorial' – but they may well have undergone some changes of reference in their new location, just as you yourself have changed in the transition to the university setting. Other terms may be entirely new to you. In addition, terminology does vary from place to place, and institution to institution, so throughout this volume we have tried to indicate our preferred terms but also the phrases and concepts they are interchangeable, or overlap, with. The index to this volume should serve as a comforter: to be consulted in times of confusion or for clarification.

If we were to imagine in a physical sense arriving in a university department, school or faculty, we might imagine you arriving in a building full of offices with names on doors – along with posters, postcards, lists of consultation hours, conference advertisements and so on – and noticeboards dotted around. You may find the noticeboard that relates to your specific year, course or module and find various bits of useful information you can write down from there, such as tutors' or lecturers' office locations and telephone numbers, the rooms in which lectures will take place and the times they will take place at, possibly even a welcoming party at which you can meet members of the department, school or faculty you have just joined. It is always a good idea in these early days to have a notebook (and pen) in which to jot down some of this information before it gets lost. Much of this information will be available in the form of handouts, possibly distributed at induction meetings or introductory lectures, and/or in handbooks published by your department, faculty or institution. In many cases, these handbooks are complemented, or in some cases substituted for, by specific homepages in the university or college websites. These are all 'sites of information', then, that it is worth familiarising yourself with in the early days of arrival. Another crucial 'site' will be the department or school office: administrative staff can provide a wealth of information on courses and often distribute course materials. You may be required by your institution to register in the office, sometimes providing a passport-sized photograph that will be kept on your individual student record file (for more details on what these record files might contain, see p. 37). Once again, find out where your departmental office is at the beginning, but bear in mind that in the first week of any academic year, the co-ordinators and staff in that office will be extremely busy. Try to be patient and understanding while you wait for your individual problem or question to be dealt with. Nearby to the main office, you will usually find the student pigeonholes – a primary means of communication between the office and students, and lecturers and students. Get into the habit early on of checking your mail on a regular basis. Your individual department will have its own recommendations as to what is 'regular' but at least once, preferably twice, a week is a good working rule. Nowadays, communication with students by email is also common; you will be advised on how to set up your email account and get hold of vital objects such as student identity cards. All of these things provide you with access to the facilities that will improve and enhance your experience of university life.

Just orientating your way around the corridors and hallways of the departmental building can seem daunting enough in those busy early days of being an undergraduate. This volume cannot replace the practical experience of identifying, walking to, and familiarising yourself with those sites and their hours and modes of operation, but it is hoped that it will serve as a useful supplement to them. You may find yourself writing down the times and locations of lectures but wondering what lectures are really like and how you should be approaching them. Using the index or list of contents in this volume should answer your questions and help you do exactly that. Similarly, you may find yourself a few weeks in with your first assignment to complete – an essay perhaps, or a presentation – and, once again, this book can help you to prepare for and carry out those assignments. Of course, it is more than likely that your own lecturers will also offer advice and guidance on the same issues – through lectures, seminars, the handbook or the website – and, in that respect, this book is a means of following up on that advice, exploring the ideas further, or just checking that you are working along the right lines.

To this end, we have divided the volume into two parts: one which looks at English literature as a discipline and aims to explain what an English literature degree is, what a course of study with this title might contain, and some of the reasons for studying the subject as well as the skills and interests you might expect to develop and hone; and another on the study skills that we have identified as crucial to the successful experience and completion of a literature degree. Each of these sections is divided into smaller sub-sections to help you negotiate your way through the material via the contents page or the index. The volume has also been designed so that each section interacts with the other and you will therefore find many areas of overlap or cross-reference. If Part One provides you with some of the concepts and theories behind the discipline, Part Two offers some coping strategies for dealing with the mechanics of studying English. Practical mechanics can often provide the means of access to the more complex theoretical aspects of a subject, just as the theories are what make the mechanics exciting: they are what the mechanics make possible, as it were. We have tried to indicate throughout the volume, therefore, where useful cross-references might be pursued, though we would also hope that

engaged readers will find many of their own. Study skills are
not separate from the disciplinary specifics of studying literature and for that reason the skills described in Part Two are
very much embedded in the picture of the subject we are trying
to paint in Part One.

We have already raised the thorny matter of terminology.
Different institutions not only have different titles (university
and college of higher education, for example) and sub-titles
(faculty, school, department, or centre), but they also deploy
different terms to describe what they do. You may study in
blocks of time referred to as terms or semesters (and the
lengths of these will vary from place to place); you may opt
on to courses or modules. The people who teach you may have
a number of titles: lecturers, tutors, teachers and facilitators
are just some of the more common of these. Your route into
the institution may also have differed: you may be entering
university via the route of further study at school post-sixteen,
in which case you may have taken A levels, or a combination
of A/S and A2 levels if you are a student in England, Wales or
Northern Ireland, and Highers, and possibly supplementary
certificates, if you are a student in Scotland. In some instances
you may have taken an alternative form of qualification such
as an International Baccalaureate. Alternatively, you may be
returning to study after a gap following school, in which case
you may be a mature student entering via an access course.
You may be intending to study in a full- or part-time capacity.
It would create a fairly unwieldy book if we tried to take into
account all of these permutations at every possible occasion
when they might apply to a given individual; so we have opted
for some basic, standard terms which readers may use to apply
to their personal situations. In this respect, we will talk in the
main of 'lecturers' and 'departments' and of sixth-form or
final-year studies at school to cover all the permutations
suggested above. It is also true to say that degree courses,
whether full or part time, can vary in length and shape as well:
while a three-year degree is at present the standard length in
England, Wales, and Northern Ireland, in Scotland, students
follow a four-year degree programme, graduating with a

Masters' rather than a Bachelors' degree as is the norm in the other locales. As already mentioned, students may also be studying English literature in combination with another subject or subjects. It is again impossible for our templates to cover every nuance and eventuality, but we have on the whole assumed the basic model of a three- to four-year programme in which students progress through the years to different and increasingly advanced levels of courses. This will not always be the case in reality either. In some institutions, courses are offered across years: that is to say that you may find yourself following a course on gothic literature in a seminar featuring first- and final-year undergraduates, some studying in a full-time capacity, others part-time, students who are not majoring (that is studying as the major part of their degree programme) in English but are taking supplementary or subsidiary modules, as well as interested members of the wider community who are taking the course as part of a programme in Continuing and Professional Education (sometimes referred to as Adult Education or Life-long Learning Programmes). Such courses do not involve the level of gradated progression that our preferred model assumes, but, in all other respects, the points we are making in the body of the book about the nature of the course or the discipline-specific skills required remain relevant.

As well as working with a template of a degree programme to keep the volume as clear and consistent as possible, we are also assuming a template student. In each section and sub-section of the volume, we do not have space or time to allow for the individual needs of students who might buy this book in order to prepare for studying for a degree in English literature. Universities are rich and varied communities of able-bodied and non-able-bodied staff and students, of shy and confident staff and students, of young and old, the sighted and the non-sighted, the hearing impaired and wheelchair users, car-drivers and bike-riders, student-parents, the dyslexic, the local and those who are visiting from overseas: that is part of the joy of being within that community. It is fair to say that individuals, often in discussion with their university admissions office, should identify specific needs that may be beyond the remit of this book to account for and deal with. If you have hearing difficulties, for example, identifying this before you arrive as an undergraduate means that note-takers and/or hearing loops in lecture halls can be organised; a student who is registered blind may be able to have handbooks in computerised form so that they can be converted into Braille or the spoken word; a dyslexic student may well be allowed extra time for comprehension and writing in examinations, and if it is helpful the examination papers along with lecture notes and handouts can be printed in alternative colours to aid reading. We are not positing an 'ideal' or 'normal' student in offering a template student in the course of our discussions and descriptions in this volume, merely offering a working model in the context of which additional needs and experiences may be identified and pursued by the individual reader and user.

At various moments in the book, we deploy actual texts – poems, novels, plays, and films from a range of historical periods and contexts – to exemplify the points we are making. While we hope that the readings we offer on texts ranging from Samuel Taylor Coleridge's poetry, Charles Dickens's *Great Expectations* and John Webster's Jacobean tragedies to Peter Carey's *Jack Maggs* will be illuminating and will offer some ideas as to how to begin to approach texts on your own modules and courses, these are not prescriptive lessons in 'how to do close reading' or 'how to read in context'. They are, rather, examples of some of the ways you might like to approach reading tasks of that kind. Once again, explore the ideas of close reading and literature in context further by exploring the books we discuss under the heading of 'Further reading'.

We hope, ultimately, that this book will prove as helpful and invaluable as all those pieces of coloured paper you will find clipped or pinned to the departmental noticeboard we were describing earlier, those which told you where to go for lectures, or for your first seminar or tutorial or workshop, and where to pick up a copy of the course handbook or the essay presentation guidelines. Having found your way through these printed corridors and noticeboards, we hope that English literature as a discipline will seem a little more familiar, a little less daunting, and as exciting, rich and stimulating as it has always seemed to us as lecturers in the subject. Getting set for university life may involve all those worries we were describing at the beginning of this introduction about kettles and computers and labelling your food in the communal fridge, but as a student of English literature it will also be about the joy of books, of reading texts across the centuries and across cultures and contexts, about discussing them, debating their ideas and aesthetics, and researching and writing about the same. What could be better?

PART I
Studying English Literature

1 WHAT IS ENGLISH LITERATURE?

What is 'English literature'? This is a question that it is helpful to ask yourself before you embark on a degree course offered in its name, leading to the qualification BA (Hons) in English Literature or English Studies (or at least a degree in which 'English' figures in the title of the award). It is possibly a question that you have never had to pose in studying A Level English, as you move from thinking about imagery in *Othello* to character in *A Passage to India*. To ask the question 'What is English literature?' is perhaps an indication of the gap that needs to be bridged between studying English at A Level, and studying English in higher education.

The question 'What is English literature?' has become a more explicit and urgent one in recent decades. It was frequently posed in the 1980s, as teachers of English in higher education especially, and secondary schools to a lesser degree, began to express a critical interest in the history of their discipline, and the assumptions that shaped the content of the subject that they taught and researched. In answering the question, they discovered that English literature was a relatively new invention in elementary, secondary and higher education. Writing in English and its linguistic precursors – Anglo-Saxon and Middle English – of course has a very long history. But it was not possible to study for a degree concerned with literature written in English until the last decades of the nineteenth century. It was at this moment that the elite universities of Oxford and Cambridge finally made provision to teach a subject that had had its origins in institutions of working-class education such as Mechanics Institutes. Given these relatively humble origins, a degree in English literature would not have been considered as valuable as a degree in the study of the original 'staples' of elite humane learning, the classical languages and literatures of Greek and Latin. If you went to study English at university – perhaps at one of the new universities designed to consolidate the civic pride of industrial centres, such as Liverpool and Manchester – you were most likely a woman for whom the rigours of the classics were considered too taxing. In studying for a degree in English literature in the late nineteenth century, a student would have encountered some of the writings that might still be found in a present-day syllabus: the Middle English narrative poetry of Chaucer, the dramas of Shakespeare, the poetry of Milton, the poetry of Pope, the critical writings of Samuel Johnson. But the student would have been unlikely to study any prose fiction by such important Victorian novelists as Charles Dickens and Charlotte Brontë: these were considered too low status, the kind of thing read during leisure, for mere pleasure. In any event, most of the writings studied would have been writings by English men.

A student studying English literature at degree level today may continue to find her- or himself studying the writings of Chaucer, Shakespeare, Milton, Pope and Johnson. All appear in options offered on the degree programme on which the authors of this book teach. But present-day students will encounter many more diverse authors, writings and objects of study, including, but not only, Charles Dickens and Charlotte Brontë. 'English literature' now also embraces literature written in the twentieth century, itself arguably a completed episode of literary history as we write from the perspective of the twenty-first century. Of course, in practice periods can never have definitively settled borders and boundaries. Witness current debates about 'the long eighteenth century' (beginning in the seventeenth century) or 'the long nineteenth century' (beginning in the late eighteenth century and ending in the early twentieth). These debates about the complex relationship between slowly developing social trends and literature contend that '1700', '1800', '1900' or '2000' are somewhat arbitrary points for organising the history of writing.

English literature can include writings in English that derive from linked countries and cultures, such as Scotland, Wales and Ireland. Indeed, it can also include writing from countries such as Australia, Canada, India, the United States and West Africa. English literature might also include literature in translation from European continental countries such as France, Germany and Italy. Such writings can be studied in themselves, or they can be studied as a part of Comparative Literature courses, in which, say, the nineteenth-century realist novel in English is compared to generically similar writings from France or Russia in the same period. Students of English literature can also now study forms of popular writing such as gothic horror and crime fiction. They may also study film and television adaptations of works that began their lives as novels or short fictions; they can study film and TV media as forms of narrative art or as forms of representation that have a sig-nificant impact on the shaping of cultural attitudes. In this respect, English has broadened its focus in response to the emergence of a new subject, cultural studies.

It was a sense of impatience with what had become a restrictively canonical version of English studies during the 1960s and 1970s that led to the broadening of the field; cultural studies emerged from this opening-out process. The term 'canonical' derives from the noun 'canon', a word that has its origins in ecclesiastical law. In literary studies, it is generally used to signify a body of writings that are strongly approved or valued. Perhaps the best-known example of canonical literary criticism can be found in the work of F. R. Leavis, whose book *The Great Tradition* (1948) argued that there were really only six English novelists that it was necessary to read. Beginning with Jane Austen and ending with D. H. Lawrence, close and serious reading of this tradi-tion would, Leavis argued, enhance the reader's complex moral perception of the world. Leavis's moral vision had a major impact on post-Second World War literary studies. At the same time, Leavis's moralism worked hand in hand with a profoundly social view of literature; the moral complexity stored up in the Great Tradition was a kind of resistance to the representations Leavis saw as saturating modern social life (such as newspapers and advertising). Thus, the social orientation of cultural studies actually emerged out of the kind of English studies bequeathed by Leavis. Many of the original practitioners of cultural studies, such as Raymond Williams, were originally teachers of English (in Williams's case, in adult education) who had been influenced by Leavis. Williams sought to extend the questions about the relationship between representations and society that had already been implicit in Leavis's teaching of English by seeking analogous sources of value in forms of art, media and culture that Leavis ignored or rejected. In other words, it has been the posing of questions that has helped to generate the sheer diversity and catholicity of the present-day discipline or subject of English. This should be stressed when answering the question, 'What is English literature?'

The present-day diversity can be seen as a response to that urgent question as it was posed in the 1980s, for it was a question that was raised in the context of an acute moment of reflexivity, or reflective self-criticism. It was the moment that coincided with the rise of literary theory. We shall discuss theory in more depth in Chapter 4. For the moment, it is enough to note that literary theory is now an important dimension of most degree courses in English literature, and perhaps the most significant difference between studying literature at A level and degree level. To that extent, theory is now a specific object of study in modules alongside modules in Renaissance Drama, or Women's Writing, or Caribbean Literature. Modularisation is a relatively new way of organising learning and teaching in British higher education (though it is by no means universal: it is not, for instance, a feature of curriculum organisation at either Oxford or Cambridge). By making units of learning and assessment self-contained and relatively autonomous, modularisation has enabled degree programmes to increase the range of choice and variety in subject matter. In the same way in which you might, in these modules, study the writings of Ben Jonson, Margaret Atwood or Derek Walcott, in a literary theory module you may study the writings of figures such as Roland Barthes, a French intellectual who was writing between the 1950s and 1970s. But whereas in a module on Women's Writing you might study selected works by Margaret Atwood, the woman author, in reading Barthes's essays 'The Death of the Author' and 'From Work to Text', you will find yourself provoked into thinking through the questions 'what is an author?', or 'what is a work of literature?' Literary theory poses questions that ask us to look closely at the common assumptions that can, if received uncritically, render a humanistic discipline restrictive. It is the particular way in which literary theory has posed questions about literature that has, in part, led to the broadening of English literature as discipline or a subject.

So, is English literature a discipline or a subject? Does it qualify as either a discipline or a subject if it can be as broad and generous and open as seemingly it is? Disciplinarity suggests rules, regularity and boundaries, and from what we have said so far, English appears to be less than willing to be bound by these. Yet, when English was first established as a degree in Oxford in 1893, the study of the history of the English language was considered to be the rigorous, disciplinary element, indeed its justification as a form of mental and moral training. A discipline is, in its most elementary form, a form of instruction, practice or exercise imparted to disciples or scholars. Thus, under the disciplinary regime of Oxford philological English, works of literature were to be imparted to pupils as 'objective' examples of English usage at any given historical period, rather than as works to be interpreted, appreciated and enjoyed. These activities were viewed as excessively 'subjective'. And yet, the subjective act of reading and enjoying literature is one of the major attractions of English literature to past and present-day students who wish to study but also become deeply involved in poetry, drama, prose, and other forms of representation. Students entering degree programmes in English literature are often asked to reflect on what they most value about the course they are about to begin. A common response is that literature is a form of study which enables them as individuals to say what they think is the meaning of a novel, play or poem; poetry is seen as the genre most open to this subjective response. The attitude can be taken too far; you may subjectively feel that Milton's *Paradise Lost* is really about a Martian invasion, but you may find it hard to persuade others to share your enthusiasm. Nonetheless, the subjective response remains an important and valid one. The subjective response to literature has its philosophical roots in a momentous shift in thinking about the human person that can be traced to the late eighteenth century. During this period, which coincided with the rise of that movement known as Romanticism, the 'inwardness' of the human person came to be valued especially highly, along with the aesthetic response of the person as 'subject'.

The rich implications of the word 'subject', and its relationship to 'subjectivity', can be usefully explored in thinking about what English literature is and the breadth of its embrace. The *Oxford English Dictionary (OED)* informs us that 'subject' has been used, since the sixteenth and seventeenth centuries, to indicate the 'subject' matter of a science or an art, as in the observation that 'all sciences have a subject, number is the subject of arithmetic'. The most basic subject matter of English literature would be writings in English. There was, however, a much earlier usage of 'subject'; from the fourteenth century, it was used to signify a person who is in the control, or under the dominion, of another, for example a lord or monarch. Practitioners of English were reminded of this usage during the 1970s and 1980s, when theoreticians such as Louis Althusser and Michel Foucault argued that human 'subjectivity' is not a free and spontaneous essence, but always constituted, in part, by forces and relations of power. It is important to bear this in mind when considering the present-day breadth and catholicity of English literature as subject matter. For instance, we can acknowledge that students of English literature now respond subjectively, not just to a Great Tradition, but to many diverse literary traditions from many different continents. But this is in part a consequence of the power relations of a colonial project that exported the English language to regions that otherwise would not have been 'subject' to the language. This project made colonised individuals into 'subjects', often by forceful imposition. The colonial project hoped that these 'subjected' individuals would come to recognise themselves through the language of 'English literature'.

It is, finally, crucial to stress that English is a multi- or interdisciplinary subject by its very nature. Literary criticism is a subject that was practised in the ancient civilisation of Greece; the philosophers Plato and Aristotle were perhaps its earliest exponents. Its 'subject matter' has evolved and developed ever since. M. H. Abrams, in an influential book entitled *The Mirror and the Lamp* (1953), observed that literary criticism had come to consist of a number of 'orientations' that foregrounded various aspects of the diverse subject matter that it addressed. Literary criticism could be oriented towards the world (or 'universe' as Abrams put it), or the audience, the author or artist, or even the work of art itself (Lodge 1972: 1–27). Abrams was formulating a quite specific argument about the transition from mimetic (or imitative) literary critical orientations – does this literary picture 'look like' the world it purports to represent, and would an audience be persuaded and instructed or pleased by it? – to more subjective artist-centred and aesthetically aware orientations (the moment of Romanticism that has been described above). Abrams's model is additionally valuable because it can give a vibrant sense of just how diverse and assimilative the subject matter of literary criticism can be. It may require that we study society, geography, politics, science, history (to situate the work in the world), or even psychology (for accounts of the author, or indeed the reading process experienced by the audience). This aspect of the subject is often doubly emphasised on dual- or joint-honours programmes, where students may be encouraged to see the links between their discrete subject areas. Even on a single-honours degree course it is important to remember that you are engaged in a subject or process that has open boundaries, one that interacts with all these crucial areas of humanistic thought and practice. English degrees regularly, and almost as a matter of course, test students' thinking, not least on what can be termed ethical issues. A student of English will graduate having not only had the opportunity to read widely but having considered questions of politics, sexuality, ethnicity and morality. These are perhaps some of the most important skills you can offer any employer, though it is also important to stress the practical skills that are honed in the process: those of independent research and thinking, ability to identify discourse and context, and skills of presentation, oral and written.

2 WHY STUDY ENGLISH LITERATURE?

A good understanding of what the benefits of your chosen university subject are can often help you in pinpointing the exact skills and attributes you should strive to acquire and to improve during your academic career. The central questions are what the subject, if you like, is *for* and the reasons why it might be valued by an employer or by society in general as a course of study.

English, English Literature and English Studies, either as single-subject degree courses or as components of combined or multi-disciplinary degree structures, have an ever increasing relevance to contemporary society. The twenty-first century is frequently referred to as the 'media' or 'communications age', and English courses both develop and ameliorate communication and interpersonal skills in varied ways. The capability of individual students to form and articulate spoken and written arguments is extended through a variety of learning situations; students are also encouraged to value the manifold benefits of team-working.

Of course, the core element of any English programme remains the training of students to respond with sensitivity and intellectual awareness to a range of literary texts and situations. There is a large degree of subjectivity and personal response implicit in this, and in stressing the mechanics of the subject we are anxious not to lose sight of these highly pleasurable aspects of study. Nevertheless, these texts will have been written in diverse genres and across historical periods and cultural boundaries and students of English are expected to acquire a range of skills that are discipline-specific in being able to recognise, identify and interrogate these aspects of a text, as well as noting a personal or subjective response to its contents.

The most obvious area under this heading in which students develop skills is often categorised as close reading (alternatively described as 'Practical Criticism' or critical appreciation). Students are aided in the development of both the confidence and the range of practical skills required to respond to any piece of literature or any cultural text placed before them, without necessarily having any previous contextual knowledge of the author or the conditions of the text's production. Genre is of especial importance in this kind of close-reading approach. Students become increasingly familiar with the conventions and traditions of particular genres – poetry, prose, drama and often, in a related or associated sense, film – but also with specific sub-genres or categories such as comedy, tragedy, pastoral, satire and gothic. These generic conventions form a kind of vocabulary or functioning toolbox that students can carry with them throughout their studies and apply whenever they are confronted by a text for analysis or comment.

The real truth that any English student learns, however, is that literature is almost always at its most interesting and exciting at that point where the standard conventions are disrupted or disturbed – at the pressure points where the novelist, playwright, poet or director consciously and innovatively subverts tradition. Shakespeare's *Sonnets* are a perfect case in point. This long sequence of fourteen-line poems clearly has a strong relationship to the sonnet tradition and form. The traditional line length and the conventional subject matter of love are observed, but Shakespeare also creates his own version of the sonnet form within that traditional structure and context. By dividing his individual sonnets into three quatrains (groups of four lines) and a rhyming couplet – the division is achieved by a combination of rhyme and metre – he fashions his own more muscular version of the sonnet form perfected by the Italian writer Petrarch. Petrarch's sonnets tended towards an octave, sestet or eight-line, six-line division, which was particularly suited to the rhythms and vocabulary of the Italian language. Shakespeare finds a poetic pattern more suited to the rhythms and stresses of English, not least

the propensity of monosyllables it contains. Within that overall structure, Shakespeare also makes frequent play with the
iambic pentameter, the traditional, or conventional, ten-syl-
lable line of English poetry. In certain lines Shakespeare adds
or removes an extra syllable for effect. By this means, he is able
to exploit the suggestive power of poetic stress. In Sonnet 20,
for example, the plethora of eleven syllable lines ensures that
each line ends in an unstressed syllable, rather than the
traditional stressed end to the English iambic pentameter.
This makes sense when we consider the subject matter of
the sonnet more closely. A figure of sexual androgyny is the
addressee: 'A woman's face with nature's own hand painted/
Hast thou, the master-mistress of my passion;' (ll. 1–2) and so
these weak (or unstressed) endings, also known as feminine
endings, actually underline the sexual confusion implicit in the
sonnet itself. Weak endings are also a clever means of suggest-
ing doubt – Hamlet's mental dilemma is conveyed in perhaps
what is the most famous of all Shakespeare's elongated eleven-
syllable lines: 'To be, or not to be; that is the question:'
(III.i.57). Conversely, truncated lines can suggest a mind
suddenly distracted and drawn to other matters, or a failure
of the thought itself, a recognition of its impossibility or
extravagance; in another *Hamlet* soliloquy, the Danish prince
considers the convincing grief of the Player King in a performance of a story from the Trojan wars, recognising the
pretence involved when he draws line 535 up short:

> Is it not monstrous that this player here,
> But in a fiction, in a dream of passion,
> Could force his soul so to his own conceit
> That from her working all his visage wanned,
> Tears in his eyes, distraction in's aspect,
> A broken voice, and his whole function suiting
> With forms to his conceit? And all for nothing.
> For Hecuba!
> What's Hecuba to him, or he to Hecuba,
> (II.ii.528–36)

This extract also contains several further examples of the eleven-syllable line and the intellectual flexibility Shakespeare achieved with this form. In line 529, the insubstantial nature of a 'dream of passion' is emphasised by the weak ending; similarly, a word such as 'nothing' carries its own lack of substance over into the extra unstressed syllable. These are just fleeting examples of what close reading can achieve in response to a text. What English literature provides students with is that aforementioned toolbox for carrying out these kinds of investigations for themselves. A common response from students in disciplines other than English literature is that English is a 'soft' subject, because they too can 'read' texts. Another much-heard statement is that interrogating or unpacking a great poem, novel, or film 'ruins' it for the reader. Neither statement is accurate. Literacy skills do not equate to skills of textual study or analysis. It is these latter skills that your toolbox is providing you with on an English programme. Nor does acquiring those skills ruin the pleasure that is embodied in the action of reading literary texts; indeed, many scholars of English literature, many of the lecturers you will debate these texts with on your courses, either in seminars or in the form of reading critical works by them in the library, would argue that it achieves the opposite, opening up a whole world of possibilities for reading and interpretation. How much *more* exciting the above-quoted Shakespeare sonnet is when you can see its theme of sexual ambiguity extended and underlined by the poetic structure of the poem; how exciting it is to realise that one of the reasons why Hamlet is so seductive as a stage character is because it is the rhythms as well as the words of his soliloquies that are having an effect on us as an audience in the theatre. The toolbox of skills that will enable you to recognise poetic strategies such as rhyme, metre or stress can help to make 'difficult' or unwieldy texts such as Edmund Spenser's lengthy Elizabethan epic *The Faerie Queene* far more accessible to the student-reader. The grammatical knowledge and awareness that will enable you to explore how and why James Joyce sheds all rules of punctuation in the monologue he writes for Molly Bloom at the close of his own prose epic *Ulysses* is anything but rigid and boring. The skill to close-read Molly's orgasmic utterances may also help you to recognise the loving pastiche of Joyce that is effected by Jonathan Coe at the close of his recent novel *The Rotter's Club* (2001). In this way, you are also adding the skills of identifying and exploring pastiche, parody and appropriation, of thinking about intertextuality, to your expanding collection of tools. What the skills give you is the means to access an ever-wider community of texts and ideas: it is an opening-out of possibilities rather than a closing-down of them. If you can then add to them the skills of contextualisation – skills that might, for example, encourage a reader to explore why Coe alludes to Joyce's urban epic set in Dublin in the context of his own attempt to write a history of 1970s Birmingham – then the possibilities, the directions open to you as a reader, multiply yet further.

As the latter invocation of Joyce and Coe indicates, it is not only poetry that is subject to this kind of close reading or unpacking of textual strategy. The novel or prose narrative more generally is equally subject to these rich and meaningful subversions of convention. Time-sequences are a common means by which an author can disrupt expectations in a novel, resisting the conventional linear plotline that would see a story progressing neatly from beginning to middle to end in an ABC-type sequence. Marina Warner's 1992 novel *Indigo* and Kate Atkinson's 1997 *Human Croquet* both deploy twisting, circular narrative forms, allowing their novels to move in and out of different time-periods and even frames of possibility. Whether these more circular narratives are forms preferred by radical or oppositional writers is a matter for debate and discussion. The writings of both Atkinson and Warner, who are women authors with an investment in feminist debate, could be ascribed deliberate patterning of this kind. Both novelists are influenced in turn by a school of writing sometimes referred to as 'magic realism' that originated in South and Central American literature. A specific political ideology can also be identified as promoting and shaping that literary technique. What is certain is that part of the personal toolbox that any English student establishes will be a sense of emergent patterns but also multiple exceptions to every rule. In this respect, the toolbox approach we are describing enables the process of 'reading in layers' that we advocate elsewhere in this volume (see Chapter 5).

Narrative or narratology is another means by which a writer, especially a writer of prose, can disturb or subvert formal conventions. A narrator might more usually be expected to impart information to a reader about the lifestyle, context or even motives of characters, but narrators, especially first-person narrators where the issue of bias is paramount and even implied by the form, can also confuse, mislead or manipulate readers. The convention of the 'unreliable narrator' as represented in a novel such as Kazuo Ishiguro's *The Remains of the Day*, where the effect of a first-person narrator looking back on their lives with a degree of guilt or wish-fulfilment actually twists the accurate portrayal of past events into more oblique and suppressive modes, is one strain of the subversion of narrative form that has provided rich material for literary criticism. Self-aware writings of this nature are often linked to a more modern mindset and in particular the school of thought entitled postmodernism, but in truth this kind of self-conscious literature is centuries old. Early modern drama was highly engaged with the ideas of metatheatre, theatre that referred to its own artificial constructs by means of tropes of disguise or plays within plays or even by means of overt structural devices such as prologues and epilogues. Drama provides yet another portfolio of conventions and structures that can provide students with helpful working templates to apply when reading or responding to playtexts.

Metafiction or metanarrative was promulgated in the eighteenth-century work of Laurence Sterne, whose brilliantly inventive and groundbreaking *The Life and Times of Tristram Shandy* is itself invoked in an act of intertextuality by Kate Atkinson's *Behind the Scenes at the Museum* (1995). Allusions to, adaptations of, and appropriations of previous works of literature have also been identified as a postmodern tendency. When these texts are adapted across cultural boundaries, such as Jean Rhys's reworking of Charlotte Brontë's *Jane Eyre* from a Caribbean perspective in *Wide Sargasso Sea* or Peter Carey's revisioning of Dickens's *Great Expectations* from an Australian viewpoint in *Jack Maggs*, the ideologies and methodologies of postcolonialism come in to play. What can further enrich the student's toolbox of approaches to literature, then, is an awareness of some of these different schools of thought, such as feminism, postmodernism and New Historicism. This kind of reading, along with aspects of what is commonly referred to as literary theory, is explored in more detail, using *Great Expectations* as an example, in Chapter 4.

As well as developing the skills of close reading and what has sometimes been referred to as reader-response techniques, students of English acquire the ability to consider and explore texts in contexts, social, political and historical. Some courses may be structured around particularly seminal events in history, such as the French Revolution and its impact on movements such as Romanticism, or the English Civil War in the seventeenth century, or the Great War at the start of the twentieth century. The 'Romanticisms' course, as well as studying canonical figures such as William Wordsworth, Samuel Taylor Coleridge, Lord Byron, John Keats, and Percy Bysshe and Mary Shelley, might seek to challenge the canon of Romantic literature by looking at less well-known or less frequently anthologised writers, including women poets, the political works of William Godwin, or popular genres such as gothic. It might also explore how a writer such as Jane Austen, who is not usually classified as a 'Romantic', relates to or interacts with these writers and styles which were after all contemporary to her own novel-writing. Students would acquire the skills to look at a range of textual and cultural productions during these time-periods and to consider how writers react or respond to events around them, but they are also invited constantly to challenge categories and labels. A questioning mind is certainly one of the greatest skills any English student can expect to develop.

Other courses might be more explicitly governed by an overall theme or topic, such as gender, race or 'utopian fictions'. Such a course might consider texts written across a range of historical moments, though context would still be relevant in each case. A course on the topic of race, for example, might include William Shakespeare's *The Tempest*; Aphra Behn's late seventeenth-century prose fiction *Oroonoko*; Daniel Defoe's eighteenth-century experiment in novel-writing, *Robinson Crusoe*; and Maria Edgeworth's 1801 *Belinda*, coming up to date with two further novels, J. M. Coetzee's *Foe* (which would provide a means of looking at the aforementioned strategies of intertextuality or appropriation since in its title the novel indicates its allusion to Defoe), and Caryl Phillips's *Cambridge*, and David Dabydeen's poem 'Hogarth' (which has its own interdisciplinary frame of reference to the visual arts). If this course operated in a New Historicist mode, these primary literary texts (which offer a cross-section of genres) might also be explored alongside non-fictional texts such as pro-abolitionist pamphlets or essays by postcolonial critics and literary critical reflections on race such as the film critic Richard Dyer's *White*. Students might deploy their toolbox of skills on this kind of course to consider how genre is adopted or subverted to support or reflect particular political positions and to challenge or manipulate reader response. They would also use the same skills of historical contextualisation that would be required on a more overtly period-based course.

The toolbox of skills then that an English literature student will acquire includes those specific to reading and interpreting texts. It would be fair to suggest that many students opt to study at university in a higher educational context because they enjoy reading literary texts and because they are reasonably adept and skilled at doing so. The question 'Why study English?' can therefore be answered in part with the response: 'because it is enjoyable and because it extends the range of reading opportunities open to me'. But this is not to deny the practical as well as pleasurable applications of the tools that students amass and learn to handle during the years of their degree studies. Through seminars and related learning situations, as well as through developing the ability to think independently (and, as we suggested in Chapter 1, ethically), students gain practice in making presentations, both oral and written. They also hone the skills of teamwork and group interaction. As a result, English graduates go into a wide range of professional vocational positions, including the obvious areas of teaching, journalism and publishing, but also routes such as arts administration, law, management, banking and finance. This occurs not least because the skills detailed above that the subject provides are multi-purpose ones, relevant to all walks of life. That these general skills of application and communication have been perfected within the context of being able to engage with some of the most exciting and challenging forms of expression available over a three- or four-year university degree simply increases the attractiveness of the subject. English literature in higher education is a key to a door that opens onto an exciting and hugely varied social landscape.

Many English courses at universities today offer options in English language as well as literature. That subject-area is covered by another volume in this series and we are focusing on literary studies in this book. However, we should stress that language and linguistics courses offer rich and stimulating counterparts to the kinds of courses and skills acquisition we are describing here. Nor should we end this chapter, without referring to the fact that an English degree also frequently introduces students to additional or extra-mural routes such as drama and creative writing, debating and journalism. Involvement in university societies or the local community can all feed into the overall English literature programme you might be following and should not be underestimated as part of the skills base you can acquire (part of that now infamous toolbox) as a university student. Why do English literature as a subject? For all these reasons and more: it is one of the best means of accessing and beginning to understand the rich fabric of our lives.

3 WHAT FORMS CAN THE STUDY OF ENGLISH LITERATURE TAKE?

This chapter is divided into two main areas: (1) learning situations and (2) assessment methods. Both areas reveal the rich diversity of situations that it is possible to encounter and experience on an English degree and both indicate the need for individual students to recognise and access the opportunities for learning and support that are available to them. Neither of the lists is exhaustive, but hopefully they provide a means of becoming familiar with terms and methods that you will meet with on a degree programme, and of developing good personal strategies in approaching them.

3.1 LEARNING AND TEACHING SITUATIONS

The diversity of learning and teaching situations in which you may find yourself on an English degree course has already been mentioned as a good reason for opting to study this discipline at university. The aim of this section is to unpack some of these situations and their potential for learning and self-development in more detail. There will be some notable differences to how things might have operated for you at school or college though there will also be many recognisable areas of overlap and continuity.

Lectures as teaching units may be one innovative element of your university study programme and there may be what seems to you a much-increased emphasis on the value of literary criticism and theory alongside your personal response to set texts. But there will also be continuity with what you have been doing in terms of study and approach on your pre-university programmes. These days, many A/A2 level or Higher courses emphasise the importance of ideas of genre and context to the study of literature and so the emphasis to be found in many university syllabuses on literature in context – social, historical and political, as well as generic – may be more familiar territory. You may well also have developed the specific skills of working in small discussion groups, so some of the approaches in university seminars or tutorials will seem logical rather than frighteningly new or strange. Assessment models will have their fair share of the familiar and the unfamiliar, and this chapter will also map out some of the approaches you can expect from this aspect of a university degree programme in English literature.

First, however, we aim to explore the different kinds of learning situation you will more than likely encounter at one time or another on your degree course:

1. seminar or tutorial
2. workshops or informal lectures
3. formal lectures
4. supervisions or individual consultations
5. feedback sessions or progress interviews
6. independent learning and research.

3.1.1 Seminar or tutorial

This form of learning and teaching situation is referred to by a variety of names: small group teaching; tutorial; seminar; class. Numbers of students in each group of this nature can vary from institution to institution and class to class, but a good working model would be a group of eight to twelve students for the small group tutorial, rising to fifteen to twenty for the larger seminar model. Duration in time of these sessions can also vary, but one to two working hours is a good basic model.

Conventionally you will have at least one seminar/tutorial a week for each course you are currently taking. On a single-honours programme you will do two or three courses simultaneously; on a dual-honours programme you might expect to follow at least one course for each principal subject at any one time. Texts for discussion and the terms for analysis in the seminars are usually established for each session at least a week in advance (and usually you are aware of what text is assigned to what week from the overall course programme handed out at the start of the term/semester). You may find yourself preparing a particular play, poem or novel for each session (and the study skills discussed in Chapter 7 gives more detailed advice on the form this preparation can take). All students in the group will be expected to have prepared the designated text and to come along with ideas for the discussion within the seminar situation itself. On occasion, tutors will assist in guiding the preparation of the set text in a more detailed way, via the provision of set questions to consider or particular passages to prepare in detail, or a worksheet to follow and prepare and to use as part of the seminar structure. You may have a presentation to give to the group, or have been asked to lead the seminar in a given week.

Naturally, the expectations of the depth and breadth of your preparations will alter as you progress through a degree programme, so that a final-year student will probably be expected to prepare a set text in far more detailed fashion, deploying secondary research and close-reading skills, than a first-year student might. You may also find that by your final year you are being asked to prepare more than one text for seminars and tutorials. This is a fair reflection of how your reading and research skills will be expected to have improved and increased by this stage in your studies.

A sample first year seminar could look something like the following. It is week four of your first semester or term at university. Your set text for that week, on a core course entitled 'Genres', is Jane Austen's *Sense and Sensibility*. In the week-three seminar, your tutor or facilitator provided you with a worksheet defining four main areas to think about when reading and preparing notes on the novel for the following week. Remember that you are likely to have had lectures and/or workshops on the novel and on Austen's career and context in general that will also aid and assist you in this preparatory task. Get all your notes on the text and its context together in a file so that you can cross-reference and make connections. Materials like lecture handouts may contain useful references for further reading that will be of great help in preparing the seminar worksheet.

The four areas of interest outlined on the seminar worksheet are:

1. Money and inheritance.
2. The concept of 'Sensibility' in the eighteenth and early nineteenth centuries.
3. The use of location and setting in the novel.
4. Narrative strategies and techniques deployed by Austen.

It is a perfectly fair and reasonable question to ask what is expected of you in preparing notes according to the distributed worksheet. Often your tutor or facilitator will explain or discuss these expectations but if you are unclear about any aspect of the assignment, then simply ask. You can do that in the seminar itself when the worksheet is handed out or by consulting your tutor in an office or consultation hour in advance of the next tutorial. It might be that a side of A4 paper full of notes will suffice as a response to the worksheet or perhaps a paragraph on each topic, depending on what else is planned for the week-four session. Read the whole novel through, making detailed notes as you go, not just on these four structuring topics, but also on other related topics or ideas that strike you. Remember that in the exam or essay assignment you cannot be sure that one of the four topics on the worksheet will come up. Select some specific passages that relate to the discussion topics and record page numbers so that you can refer to them quickly and easily in the seminar situation (this also means that fellow students can follow your point in their own texts). For example, you might wish to draw attention to the opening of the novel with reference to topic 1 and the theme of disinheritance or dispossession. In the novel, we see the female protagonists losing their family home due to

the law of primogeniture, which regarded male heirs as pre-
dominant in families at this time. Concepts of houses, the
notion of home and property are also crucial to those same
protagonists when thinking about the significance of setting
and location in the novel (topic 3). With these kinds of
structured notes in front of you, you will be able to make
the most of the seminar on *Sense and Sensibility*. You should
feel confident enough to offer interventions in debates and
discussions and be able to find what you are referring to with
ease. Make sure you don't assume all the work is done by the
time of the seminar, however. Listening to other students will
test and refine your own approaches and perhaps draw your
attention to ideas that hadn't initially occurred to you. So take
notes within the seminar session and remember to look at
these after the session and follow up any ideas or concerns,
perhaps with further reading and research in the library. This
will prove invaluable to you when you come to write an
assessed essay or revise for a formal examination on the
course. For more details on how to prepare for and use a
tutorial, see Chapter 7.

Of course, the extended example we have given here is of a
first-year seminar; a final-year seminar might be rather different. The seminar itself might be longer and two texts or
more might be set for comparative discussion. A sample final-
year seminar on the US author Joyce Carol Oates might elect
to study her novels *Black Water* and *Blonde*, both of which
deploy historical 'fact' in a fictional context (the former dealing with the Chappaquidick drowning of Mary-Jo Kopechne
involving Senator Edward Kennedy and the latter the life story
and film career of Marilyn Monroe).

  The week-three seminar on Oates is prepared for by a sheet
of paper distributed to students identifying some possible
areas for exploration. Because this is aimed at final-year
students, the approach is possibly less prescriptive than might
be used for first-year students, who are still establishing their
skills in the discipline. But a structure is implicit nevertheless:
students are asked to read both novels (since they are long

novels, they have known since the beginning of the semester that they should be getting on with this and not leave it all until week three). They are also asked to make detailed notes, bearing in mind the following areas of interest: synecdoche; history; film and narrative. In addition, they are set the task of looking at secondary material on Joyce Carol Oates and coming up with at least one article or chapter in a book or journal that they can recommend to the group. One student agrees to a do a five-minute presentation on the Chappaqui-dick story, so that all students will be up to speed on that particular event in contemporary US history and another elects to explore reviews of the novels concerned. The tutor offers to bring along some clips of specific Monroe films that will be interesting to view in relation to specific passages in *Blonde* in the seminar the following week.

You will begin to see how the element of individual research has increased by this stage of a student's degree career and how the structure and approach to seminars shifts accord-ingly. A degree course is a learning curve and if anything seems strange or difficult at first, you can take comfort in the knowledge that you will develop the skills and the strategies to be carrying out work of this level by your final year.

3.1.2 Workshops and informal lectures

These forms of learning and teaching situations are increas-ingly common on degree programmes and tend to accommo-date work in group sizes that are larger than a basic tutorial but smaller than the large-lecture situation, which may de-mand a more formal style of teaching or information provi-sion. Workshops or smaller group lectures are often more structured and less openly discursive than seminars and can accommodate students of groups of 20–40. Within this larger group setting, however, you will frequently be divided into smaller sub-groups of five to six students for the purposes of particular exercises. As with the tutorial/seminar, you will usually have a set purpose for the session, often a focus text or texts (comparative work is frequently an element of workshops, enabling students to make the informed connections between two or more texts that exam and essay questions regularly demand of them). Sometimes a specific passage or passages will have been assigned to students for preparation to enable the workshop to pursue close reading or close analysis of those extracts without having to assign over a huge chunk of the time to reading the passage concerned. The idea, as with the worksheet provision described in section 3.1.1, is that students come ready prepared for the discussion: it is the most economic use that can be made of the precious learning and interactive space of the seminar or workshop. Sometimes additional secondary or theoretical reading might also have been set that can help inform or guide the discussions.

A second-year workshop on Aphra Behn's seventeenth-century prose fiction *Oroonoko*, for example, might pursue the following structure. A preparatory worksheet was distributed in week eight for the week-nine workshop. It has asked you to read the work in detail but also to concentrate in your preparatory notes on the following areas for discussion, posing specific questions and tasks in relation to them:

1. First-person narrative – explore the concept of the 'unreliable narrator' in prose fiction.
2. Genre – *Oroonoko* is a complex text that evokes relations with fiction, history, romance, drama and travel narrative. Find at least five passages that evoke different forms of generic context and convention that we can look at in the session.
3. Topic of slavery.
4. The representation of the 'hero'. Prepare a detailed close reading of pages 80–1 of the text.

It is pretty clear from this what is expected of you. When you arrive for the week-nine workshop, students can divide into sub-groups to look at either section 1, 2, 3 or 4, since they have all prepared the material. The tutor may create four groups, each to look at one of the sections and then bring the group back together as a whole at a certain point in the workshop to share ideas. Another common technique in large group teaching is to use the snowball effect – this is where students start in very small groups, possibly even pairs, and then convey the essence of their discussions to a slightly larger group and so on until the whole group comes back together at the end. It is easy to understand how by working in this way not only does the sometimes inhibiting presence of lots of students get counteracted by small group work, but lots of material can get covered very efficiently. If one big group tried to discuss a topic it could get unwieldy and some students might dominate while others fell silent. This way, the maximum number of views and topics gets heard and examined.

In addition to this kind of buzz-group work, students may also give presentations, either as individuals or as groups, on assigned topics; they may lead the workshop in a given week, which could mean focusing on a particular area of interest or using structured questions to facilitate discussion as a whole group. Book reviews are also a common form of assignment that enables students to access secondary reading carried out by others and assess for themselves what material may be useful or salient for their own studies.

Another possible structure for this form of learning situation would be the analysis of film or performance sequences.

For example, a final-year session on Baz Luhrmann's 1996 film *William Shakespeare's Romeo + Juliet* might look like this:

Students have been instructed to watch the film in advance of a week-eight session. In week seven, they explored the source text for the film, William Shakespeare's play of the same name, in some detail, including an analysis of the scene where Romeo and Juliet first meet during the masked ball at the Capulet family home (Act I, scene v). Students have discovered from studying the play's dramatic verse that the lovers meet over a shared sonnet (ll. 90–103) and the poetic 'music' of Shakespeare's play has been considered. For week eight, the tutor has also set as required reading an article by a film critic on the use of music in the film. All the students are expected to read this in advance of the session.

At the start of the session, the tutor shows the sequence from the film where Romeo and Juliet meet at the masked ball. The clip is shown twice: on the first occasion, students can simply watch, on the second occasion they take notes, recording their observations about such issues as music, lyric, cinematography, *mise-en-scène*, spatiality, editing, lighting and costume. The tutor then divides the group into four small groups to share their responses. One person is elected as note-taker and another as presenter – the person who will summarise their ideas to the group. The shared nature of the learning process is very clear.

After ten minutes working in groups, the whole class then spends fifteen minutes sharing ideas and watching the sequence a further time to confirm and evidence points raised. The whole process is then repeated, this time examining a sequence from the film involving Mercutio and recitation of the 'Queen Mab' speech at I.v.55–103. The tutor stresses at the close of the session that students now have a template for examining in detail other sequences within the play and film in the context of their own independent studies. The value of sharing knowledge, testing different approaches to texts, and models of participation and co-operation within the context of workshop learning is made clear to all the students involved.

3.1.3 Formal lectures

The formal lecture is likely to be the mode of teaching least familiar to students making the transition from A Levels/ Highers or equivalent access courses to university. As Chapter 6 on lectures explains, lectures can be a highly efficient means or mode of imparting crucial or basic information to a large body of students. They can also be particularly effective in providing students with a detailed understanding of the historical and critical contexts of the literary texts they will be or have been discussing in detail in seminars or workshops. Lectures provide, if you like, the macro-approach that complements the micro-approach of the close readings and detailed discussions that are possible in seminars, informing and nuancing those same discussions.

Increasingly at university, lectures are less passive instruments of learning than active and engaged situations. Students should always read any focus text or passage in advance of a lecture, just as they would for a seminar. Lecturers will assume a basic knowledge of the text that they are contextualising and describing: the purpose of a lecture is never to inform you of plot or content in advance of reading; it is to provide modes and means of analysis that will enhance your studies. A detailed knowledge of the text or texts, or even period, under discussion will allow students to engage with the material in the lecture in a more informed way, as well as to ask and respond to questions and queries. Someone describing to you the significance of scenic juxtaposition in a play you have neither watched nor read will of course seem 'boring', but if you already have some ideas about, and responses to, the play in hand, you will be able to make a genuine assessment of these claims. A crucial part of 'getting set' for university study is to realise the value of lecture courses and to approach them with the same care and level of preparation that you would the individual seminar. Just because you may not be 'assessed' on lecture performance as you might on tutorials, do not underestimate their importance to your learning career. Work hard to get the most out of lectures: prepare, ask questions and follow up ideas or new-found approaches after the lecture itself.

Lectures are usually about fifty minutes in duration, enabling you to get there five minutes after finishing a previous teaching session and to reach your next teaching session, if it is scheduled for the session immediately afterwards in the timetable, in the five minutes at the close. The size of lectures and lecture-halls can vary widely depending on the size of your department or school, whether the course is compulsory or optional, and course uptakes. Some lectures can contain as many as 200 students, others as few as 30. Many lecturers will break up the fifty minutes of the lecture into sections: they may indicate this by giving each section a title and asking for questions or reactions at the end of each. One section may involve buzz groups or discussions in pairs. Sometimes if lecturers have shown a sequence from a film or play, analysis of that sequence will form part of the lecture. Lecturers will use visual aids such as transparencies on an overhead projector (often referred to as 'OHPs'), slides, Powerpoint displays and whiteboards; they may also distribute handouts to which they will make reference in the course of the discussion. The study skills chapter on taking lecture notes (Chapter 6) examines in more detail how to deploy and respond to these approaches and materials, but here we will outline sample versions of lecture structures to assist you in thinking about what to expect in this type of learning situation.

In the examples, the course we are looking at is a Year One optional course on 'Renaissance Tragedy'. The textual material on the course is therefore concentrated on Elizabethan, Jacobean and Caroline drama and involves plays by Shakespeare, Christopher Marlowe, Thomas Middleton, John Ford, John Webster and others. The particular lectures we are exploring in the examples include a thematic lecture, which is to say one that concentrates on a topic that is common to a number of plays across the course (in this instance, the topic of family) and a lecture on the work of a specific dramatist studied on the course. Other lectures on the course may elect to discuss additional connecting topics, such as politics or religion, or provide contextual material on the theatres of the time and practical staging elements such as boy actors, costumes, stage properties or 'props', and scenery. Some will be detailed considerations of specific set texts such as Shakespeare's *Hamlet* or Ford's *'Tis Pity She's a Whore*. The course as a whole, then, offers students several different models of what a lecture can offer them in terms of learning and approach.

*

The first sample lecture is on 'Family Tragedy'. The lecture is divided into thirds. The first third provides general contextual material for the overarching theme of family, exploring what 'family' could mean to the early modern period and thinking about the significance of the Royal Family at the time. The lecture handout offers some useful structuring quotes on this topic and the lecturer uses various paintings and portraits to exemplify the points. These are shown in the lecture forum in slide form and students are encouraged to look at certain related books containing similar images in the library – these are also listed on the lecture handout under 'Further reading'.

The lecturer introduces the audience to a specific keyword that may not yet be familiar to them: iconography. This is a useful term for thinking about the symbolic significance of the images that they have just been looking at. A connection is drawn between this kind of iconography and the need to think about stage pictures and what the stage looks like at a given moment in a focus play. The relevance to the genre under discussion – drama – is stressed. Students are therefore being given in this section historical and contextual detail, not least a means of referring plays to other artistic examples from the period such as art and music, but also some keywords and approaches to apply when looking at individual plays or texts. This is an important means of indicating the value of lectures: you are not meant to learn them off by heart and simply reproduce their arguments but to recognise in them multiple future possibilities for approach and argumentation. Different lecturers will offer you different critical voices and approaches, some of which will suit your personal methods more than others. Some will have a very specific critical approach, picking up on different critical schools of thought, a number of which are outlined in more detail in Chapter 4, such as New Historicism, cultural materialism, or feminism.

The second third chooses as its shaping subject one particular set of family relations: parents and children. Furnishing examples from a range of texts on the course, including Shakespeare's *King Lear*, Webster's *The White Devil* and Shakespeare's *Othello*, different kinds of parent–child relationships are explored. The handout once again offers particular quotations for discussion and analysis. At one point the student audience is asked to add into the discussion other relationships from plays they have studied by calling them out; this is an example of what we have referred to elsewhere as an active mode of learning. A clip is also shown of a production of *King Lear*, focusing on the opening scene and the test by Lear of his daughters; the complicated relationship between family and state in this play, and in Lear's relationship with his daughters, is in this way raised via an open discussion with the audience.

The final third of the lecture concentrates on siblings and again a range of plays are invoked in the course of the discussion including *King Lear*, Middleton's *Women Beware Women*, and Webster's *The Duchess of Malfi* and *The White Devil*. The students have not yet studied these plays but the lecturer stresses that now they can bear in mind the issues of family and politics that the lecture has been unpacking when they come to prepare for and discuss these texts in seminars. The last few minutes are used to draw the students' attention to the texts for further reading recommended on the handout and to answer any questions the audience might have.

The second sample lecture from the 'Renaissance Tragedy' course is on Webster's *The White Devil*. This lecture takes a slightly different tack and decides to hone in one specific playwright's approach and an example play. Students are looking at two Webster plays on this course – *The White Devil* and *The Duchess of Malfi* – and they have already had lectures, such as the one outlined above on 'Family Tragedy', that mentioned the plays in passing. This lecture has been scheduled to coincide with the week when students are studying Webster's plays in their seminars, so by now the lecturer does assume they have a detailed understanding of *The White Devil*. This discussion will be more detailed and complex therefore than the references made in the 'Family Tragedy' lecture.

Once again the lecture is in three sections. The first third talks a little about Webster himself, showing a clip from the 1996 film *Shakespeare in Love* (dir. John Madden) that depicts Webster as a bloodthirsty young man feeding live rats to his cat and praising Shakespeare's bloodiest tragedy *Titus Andronicus*. But it also seeks to put Webster in context in terms of the artistic movements of his day, making specific links to movements in art history such as the baroque and mannerism, and using slides and transparencies to illustrate these points. The concentration on violence and corruption in Webster's plays is given an intellectual and philosophical context, and students are again encouraged to think about stage pictures and stage tableaux, picking up points and suggestions made in earlier lectures.

The second section looks at the role of the court in Webster's play and special attention is given to the double sense of the term, looking therefore at the stereotypical corrupt Renaissance court (and comparing it to those in other texts on the course, in particular in other plays by Webster and Middleton), and exploring in detail the central scene of the trial of Vittoria. Students are again given practice in scenic analysis that they can apply to other parts of the play and other playtexts.

The third section concentrates on Webster's depictions of death and spectacular violence in his plays. This connects back to the opening section on the baroque movement and the need to identify stage visuals. Students are asked to come up with a list of five salient moments in *The White Devil* that deal with death or violence and then some individual students are invited to share their lists with the whole lecture group. Connections are also drawn to texts by other playwrights on the course and students are invited to see how through further reading they can continue the thinking process on this and related matters.

These are just two examples from a single course, but they are intended to indicate the way in which lecture programmes do invariably connect and cohere into a carefully thought-out series. It is good advice to attend regularly so that you can benefit from the progression of ideas from lecture to lecture, and to be prepared for those lectures where it has been indicated that knowledge of the text or texts will be assumed. Lectures can be as many and as varied as the courses and options you pursue during your university degree. Some might offer surveys of particular periods such as the Romantic era or of specific literary movements such as modernism. Others might involve a close reading of a single poem such as Coleridge's 'Frost at Midnight' or T. S. Eliot's 'The Love Song of J. Alfred Prufrock'. Some will explore and interrogate critical approaches to a particular text, such as Jane Austen's *Sense and Sensibility* or Charles Dickens's *Great Expectations*, or a school of theory *per se* such as postmodernism or postcolonialism. The best practice is not to treat them as discrete or even self-contained events – look back over lecture notes, pursue further reading in the library, ask your lecturer questions and make links across courses and across fields of study. It is in just this way that your own independent critical voice, one of the real joys of studying this subject at the highest levels, will begin to emerge with genuine confidence and force.

3.1.4 Supervisions and individual consultations

Some institutions operate a supervisory system of teaching and in universities and colleges such as this that may well prove to be the more common learning situation for English students than the seminar and workshop models described above. Supervisions usually involve one or two students but will focus around set texts and set topics in much the same way as a seminar or tutorial. Sometimes a student's essay or written work will form the basis of the discussion. As with seminars or tutorials, it is important to establish exactly what is required of you in advance of a supervision: be sure of what to prepare and the terms on which this preparation should take place – a supervisor may provide worksheets or preparatory guideline questions in a manner akin to a tutor on a seminar-based course. Be aware of what to bring to the session and, again, as with tutorials and seminars, it is important to understand how to follow up the work done in the supervision: this may be through further critical reading or by returning to the set text in the light of the discussions you have been involved in and revising your original notes and responses accordingly.

Many students in their final year of an English degree will opt to take at least one dissertation option. Some may also have this option earlier in their degree programmes. Researching and writing a dissertation will usually bring students into contact with the individual supervision or consultation as a method of instruction. Dissertations are by their very nature highly individual projects so it makes best sense to discuss these individually with your tutor, though at various times you may be asked to present elements or an overview of your work to fellow dissertation students as a means of sharing good practice and innovative approaches. Try to use these consultation periods in an informed and structured manner. Simply turning up and hoping to 'get ideas' is not in your best interest. You may like to make a list of questions to discuss with your tutor or to provide a small piece of writing in draft form to form the basis of discussion. Tutors are usually more than willing to look at work in this way, but remember to get the work to them in good time in advance of your booked session: dropping it off an hour before is not good enough, since your tutor will invariably have other students to see or tutorial sessions to conduct. This is a good working rule for all your assignments during your studies: recognise deadlines, respect how busy your tutor is, and things will flow far more easily. Students are, of course, all individuals and some prefer regular contact concerning an assignment such as a dissertation (weekly meetings) while others prefer more staggered input from tutors. Provided you meet the requirements of the course concerned, it is perfectly acceptable for you to establish a programme that suits your learning style in agreement with the tutor concerned. Dissertations are, like any assignment, hugely improved by good time management (see Chapter 8) and a regular series of supervisions or individual consultations may prove a very helpful way of structuring and timetabling your work towards the final finished project.

3.1.5 Feedback sessions and progress interviews

One really crucial element of any degree is learning from each assignment as you go along. That means seeking genuine feedback and evaluation of each piece of work you produce, each presentation you give, each essay you write, or each examination paper you complete. Course tutors and Directors of Studies will offer regular feedback sessions in which they will be able to discuss with you how written assignments or presentations went and highlight strengths and weaknesses or areas for focus and consideration. Feedback should never be viewed simply as 'getting your mark back'. Your mark or classification is only one indicator of your performance on a course and it is from the detailed comments that tutors and markers make on essay and exam scripts that you can learn most about how to address your skills in, and approaches to, the discipline. Many degree results are built up from a collection of marks achieved over 2–3 years of a course. It is meant to be a process in which you can steadily improve, benefiting from what is called formative (that is to say, built up as you go along, allowing you to learn from mistakes and build on strengths) rather than summative (assessed entirely at the end) assessment. Don't assume that just because an exam is over and done with that you cannot learn something from the experience that will prove highly valuable when sitting your next examination paper. It might be something as simple as sticking to the question or writing an essay plan, or something more structural such as the need for close reading as well as general survey in the body of your answers. It may be as basic as writing more slowly so that the marker can fully appreciate and understand your work, or attending to poor spelling by allowing time within the exam to make corrections, as well as focusing revision accordingly. In terms of essay feedback, problems with referencing or attribution of ideas can be addressed before they develop into the more serious charge of plagiarism (see pp. 115–16), but tutors can also help with how to write good introductions or conclusions, how to think about the function and operation of paragraphs, or how to use internal quotations. Feedback is part of the structured learning programme of your degree and students who make active use of its availability invariably improve at a far faster rate than their peers.

Feedback is usually given on a specific assignment such as an assessed essay, exam or oral presentation and therefore timetabled at specific points or stages in the academic year. But there are several alternative means of seeking structured advice on your studies. In most institutions, you will be assigned a Personal or Year Tutor who can help you consider your progress on the course more generally. Many will offer progress reviews or interviews as a matter of course, but you are also free to ask for these from tutors. They often deploy items of information like feedback sheets and student records, including tutorial reports, in discussing your progress with you. These interviews or annual reviews can be a means to target particular strengths or skills. You may, for example, have a real strength in independent research, which may in turn help you in deciding whether to opt for that second dissertation element in the final year. They can also address weaknesses: for example, poor understanding of grammar may be holding your essay marks down; better planning in exams might make for more structured answers. Such discussions should not be solely marks driven either: progress interviews are a way of thinking about tutorial performance and your contribution to life at university. If you are shy, you might get some advice on confidence building; if you are nervous about doing oral presentations, the tutor will be able to suggest coping strategies. On a more general pastoral note, these interviews can also be an opportunity to raise any other problems you might be having: stress- or exam-based anxiety, loneliness or poor time management. Your course tutor may not always be the best person to deal with those problems, but they will be happy to suggest other individuals or sections of the university to contact in respect of them: people such as university counsellors, learning support officers or student welfare officers. The best lesson any student at university can learn is to never be afraid to get advice or help, and always to seek it as soon as possible.

3.1.6 Independent research

Independent research is an important skill to develop during your years at university and it is one that employers often think very highly of. Dissertation courses are designed to exploit a student's potential for independent research to the full: dissertation topics or titles are usually sourced by the students themselves and the research relies on individual skills in the library and in amassing and selecting material. Despite its title, however, independent research is often best conducted within a framework of structured advice: your dissertation tutor or supervisor is the best person to provide this in the case of a dissertation; course tutors or module convenors in most other instances. This structured advice might include suggestions for further reading or modes of research; a timetable for the research and a clear identification of required outcomes; or a series of regular meetings and consultations to reassure individual students that they are pursuing the right lines of research. As with questions of feedback and progress discussed in the previous section, we would suggest that you make full use of the help and advice that is available within any department or institution. Part of being truly independent in your thinking will be reaching the realisation that you will have to seek out help and advice in a proactive manner and not simply expect your tutor to arrange to see you. Most students appreciate the fact that university is necessarily a less prescriptive mode of learning than school, but it can also be quite a steep learning curve to realise that masses of help and advice are waiting to be accessed by the individual. Don't disappear into the ether: learn to ask questions, book appointments and keep them, and get the very best out of your studies that you can.

As a final note, it is also worth recalling in these days of government accountability and research assessment exercises that most of your tutors will be heavily involved themselves in personal research. This may sometimes mean they are not automatically available to see to your needs: they may be away working in archives or at a conference, or even on sabbatical leave, which is their opportunity to write all the books and articles you benefit from as a literature undergraduate. There is then a need to be understanding and to be organised; try to make appointments rather than turning up on the off-chance. The flip-side of this is that your tutors are doing complicated and engaged research all the time: this means they can give you the most up-to-date teaching and ideas and that they will understand exactly what you are going through when trying to write that long essay or dissertation.

3.2 ASSESSMENT METHODS

Like the subject or discipline of English *per se*, methods and modes of assessment, as well as learning and teaching, are likely to be highly varied in their range, approach, aims and objectives. As explained elsewhere in this book, such things as tutorial performance may well form part of the assessment methods of modules and courses you opt for during your degree. Oral presentations, made in groups or by individuals, are also increasingly common elements. In terms of written assessments, students may perform tasks ranging from the formal essay and related assignments such as essay plans or drafts, structured notes, writing or research portfolios, close readings or textual analyses, literature reviews and book reviews, through to the full-scale dissertation. The formal examination is another common mode of written assignment and assessment on degree courses. This might take the shape of an open-book or closed-book paper, or even a seen paper in the case of some film- or performance-based courses. It may involve essay-based answers or close analysis of passages and extracts provided on the exam paper itself. This section will try to describe in brief some of the most common forms of assignment you can expect to encounter on your degree programme. A more detailed description of the study skills required by each is offered in the study skills section of this book (see Part Two).

The areas of written assessment for consideration are:

1. essays
2. essay plans and drafts
3. writing and research portfolios, course diaries
4. close readings
5. literature reviews
6. book reviews
7. dissertations
8. examinations.

Other elements of assessment for consideration are:

 9. tutorial performance
10. oral presentations
11. peer assessment.

3.2.1 Essays

Essays will be familiar modes of assessment from your pre-university experiences, although some of the requirements and approaches may differ. Part Two offers a detailed account of how to research and write an essay in Chapter 9. One important shift may be the need to deploy and evidence the deployment of secondary criticism. Bibliographies and careful referencing can often be a steep learning curve for under-graduates, so it is worth spending some time becoming accustomed to them as practices in the first year.

Essay assignments should be exciting, so try to choose a topic or title that interests and stimulates you. Allow enough time to do the exercise justice and allow for secondary reading and research. Be ambitious rather than doing the bare minimum: this will always pay off in the final essay. If you have any concerns about writing an essay, there are various books that offer advice and help and we have recommended several of these under the heading of 'Further reading' at the back of this volume.

The required length of these assignments can vary hugely from course to course so it will be important to check the specific requirements for each assignment. A short essay may be as little as 1,500 words and an extended essay as much as 6,000 to 7,500. Word limits are important and have been decided on for good reason, so make sure you stick to them. Choose any question or title with care and seek advice or clarification from a tutor where necessary. Stick to deadlines and present essays with due care and attention, paying special care to observe any departmental or institutional regulations concerning style.

3.2.2 Essay plans and drafts

Some courses require that students present essay plans or drafts for the tutor's consideration and these may or may not be marked towards the final assessment. It is important to develop the skill of careful planning and many departments will offer lectures or advice on how to do this. A few sentences saying what you will discuss is not enough: a plan can be as much as two sides of A4 detailing points and stages in the argument, passages or extracts for close analysis and the secondary material that will be invoked and deployed. Learning to plan and draft essays, sometimes in several forms, even if they are not formally assessed, is an important skill and will improve the final essay no end.

3.2.3 Writing and research portfolios, course diaries

Some courses may include an assignment that involves the amassing of a portfolio of work during the course of a semester or term or the length of the relevant module. As well as being a clear means of evidencing your individual progress through the course, these can be a means of focusing on weak areas in advance of final or summative assessments. A student with essay-writing difficulties might use a writing portfolio to practise writing introductions or formulating paragraphs. These methods of assessment are also crucial for self-evaluation. It is important that students are active in planning their own personal development and thinking through their own progress through a degree, and portfolios or course diaries which explore and assess what is being learned, how and why, can be invaluable tools in this process. You might like to use some of the things you learn or identify about yourself in progress reviews with tutors or in feedback sessions (see p. 37).

3.2.4 Close readings

Close-reading assignments or textual analyses are sometimes given formal titles such as 'Practical Criticism' or 'Critical Appreciation'. In essence, they involve a poem, a passage of prose, or an extract from a play, which students are asked to examine in detail, paying equal attention to both form and content. These can be set as essay-based or exam-based assignments. For essays, obviously students have the opportunity to consult readings of the same text in books and articles, but it will be important to strive to achieve something original or innovative in your approach. In an exam-based assignment, sometimes students will have the text for analysis in advance of the exam, in which case the same point applies, or they may be given the text 'cold' in the exam. Some lecturers will refer to these extracts or passages as 'gobbets': this is simply a literary phrase to refer to a section of text. The passage or text in the exam may or may not be a text you have previously examined in seminars or tutorials. In such cases, the student is being assessed on an ability to bring to bear strategies and skills in reading and analysis that he or she has been developing. It is a context in which the much-mentioned toolbox of skills comes to the fore.

It may be that the text invokes a particular genre or sub-genre, such as the 'Conversational Ode' or the sonnet, that the student can invoke and explore, or that it exemplifies a particular strategy, such as the unreliable first-person narrator or the dramatic soliloquy or overhearing scene. In all cases, careful note-taking and planning is as relevant as in writing an essay-based answer. Don't rush at an assignment of this nature: it will benefit from careful teasing out of the intricate possibilities of the text in front of you. And, like so much else we have been discussing here, it is a technique you will improve at as your degree career continues. What is crucial is that you do not just describe the content of the passage before you: part of what defines literature students is their ability to respond to and extrapolate from the different forms and strategies that literature adopts and it is crucial that any critical appreciation recognises and exploits this. For more on exam preparation and revision, see Chapter 11.

3.2.5 Literature reviews

Literature reviews are sometimes also referred to as biblio-graphical exercises. Essentially, this assignment asks students to research and establish a reading list or a bibliography of texts on a particular topic, text or author. It is designed to develop skills that will be needed in researching a formal academic essay or dissertation as well as offering practice in the art of referencing and presentation stressed elsewhere in the skills section of this book.

3.2.6 Book reviews

You may be asked to complete one or more book reviews as part of your assessment requirements on a course. A book review is a rather different animal to a formal essay and in some ways one that many students enjoy because it is a chance to be polemical and subjective in a way that is more suppressed by the formal requirements of an extended essay or dissertation. Experience in writing or establishing the tone of a review can be gained by reading reviews in newspapers, magazines and journals (of course, this is also a wonderful way of keeping up with new books and ideas relevant to your course of study): the *Times Literary Supplement*, *London Review of Books*, *New York Review of Books* or review sections in newspapers such as *The Guardian* can all be excellent sources. One important skill of any English course is learning that different modes of discourse suit different situations: the approach of a book review is different to that of an essay, just as a report to a company would be different to an article in the student newspaper. The approach of a review may not be helpful, might indeed be damaging, in the context of a literary dissertation, but the ability of recognising the specific demands of this assignment when writing it will gain marks in itself.

3.2.7 Dissertations

Dissertations are discussed in more detail in Chapter 10 of this book. As with essays, these can vary hugely in length from 7,500 words to 12,000 words or more on an undergraduate programme. They are usually a product of independent research (see p. 38) and consultation with tutors and/or supervisors (see p. 34). They are usually really important modes of assignment for those students who are beginning to think about carrying on their studies to a postgraduate level as they indicate that you have begun the process of developing the skills of detailed research.

3.2.8 Examinations

This is not a mode that will be unfamiliar after school or college, but there may be significant differences in the shape or form that individual examinations take. Some students are shocked to find that they cannot take books into examinations with them; others encounter seen papers (which are issued in advance of examinations at an agreed time and date to all students, sometimes to facilitate work such as film or performance analysis or critical reading to feature in the paper) for the first time. As with all the methods of assessment outlined here, it is important for students to establish the particular requirements of each individual exam and to attend to these in preparing for and revising for the paper itself. And, as with all the assessments outlined here, it is crucial to seek feedback on what went well and what could be improved upon next time. For more detailed advice on examination preparation, see Chapter 11.

Below are other possible modes of assessment that you may encounter.

3.2.9 Tutorial performance

Tutorial performance is increasingly appearing as a mode of assessment in university courses. Ways to approach and prepare for this are discussed in more detail on pages 82–5. Under this heading it is worth thinking about not only attendance and preparation but also participation, and this can mean listening to and responding to your peers as much as having a lot to say.

3.2.10 Oral presentations

This is another common item on many English courses, where there is an understandable stress on skills of articulation and communication. It is also a skill that employers value, so it is worth developing a reputation for giving solid, accessible, clear and cogent presentations. A more detailed discussion of how to develop these skills can be found at p. 89 of this book.

3.2.11 Peer assessment

It may not always be your tutor who assesses your work. You may be asked to assess the work of fellow students and for them to assess your contributions at various stages. Such assessments may or may not count towards a final mark on any course or module. These assignments should be seen as a means of establishing a clear understanding of what you look for in assessing a good essay or presentation, which should in turn enable you to apply those same criteria to improving and enhancing your own work.

This is necessarily an abbreviated account of assessment methods on English programmes but should at least offer you a sense of the sheer range and variety of assignments you might be set. It should also make clear the developmental nature of many English degrees – all of these modes of assessment are designed to enable you to improve and extend your skills as you progress through the degree. Seeking advice and feedback, comparing one assignment with another, trying to review your own progress and development, will all mean that by your final year what might have seemed difficult assignments now appear entirely manageable and, indeed, even enjoyable.

4 THE PLACE OF 'THEORY' IN ENGLISH LITERATURE PROGRAMMES

4.1 CHRONOLOGY AND MODULARITY

We stressed in Chapter 1 the sheer diversity and catholicity of English as a subject, and in the previous section, the variety of teaching and learning situations in which undergraduate students of English may find themselves. This variety is further reflected in the wide variety of programmes that are offered by British institutions of higher education, which in turn makes it difficult to be too prescriptive in describing what an 'average' course in English might look like. This is especially so in the light of a modularised higher education system. Before modularity and literary theory, there probably was a greater degree of uniformity in English literature courses throughout Britain, a uniformity that was shaped by a received sense of chronology and literary history. Of course, there have always been variations in the duration of courses: students of English in Scottish universities take four years to complete their degrees, pursuing an honours scheme only from year three of their studies. Despite these variations, students of English might once have trodden a fairly uniform path. Students entering the first year of their degree would have taken a generalised introductory course or courses. They might then have been taken on a chronological tour of literary history from Medieval English, or even Anglo-Saxon in some instances, to the twentieth century. In between, the Renaissance, seventeenth century, eighteenth century, Romantic and Victorian periods would have been surveyed. Students might have worked on a special subject, possibly a period or an author in depth, in their final year. In addition they may even have studied a specialised course in the history of literary criticism, or have acquired some hands-on experience of close reading (the 'practical criticism' of poetry or extracts of prose). Of course, under some schemes, genre might have been the organising principle, but the study of poetry, or the novel, or drama, would still have been taught with reference to chronological assumptions.

Modularity has tended to break down chronology as the principal way of organising progression in English literature courses. In the interests of programme flexibility and extending choice, students can find themselves studying Middle English romances and postmodern twentieth-century metafictions during the same semester. This, incidentally, is not as outlandish as it may appear: studying one of Chaucer's framed narratives alongside Umberto Eco's postmodern detective story set in medieval Europe, *The Name of the Rose*, can be illuminating. There is a possible disadvantage to the waning of chronology: students probably do not acquire such a well-developed sense of literary historical succession as once they did. It is useful to map a sense of literary history through knowing that Chaucer died in 1400 and Dryden died in 1700, but there are, as we have seen in Chapter 1, important intellectual reasons for interrogating the idea of 'the period', and downplaying the importance of century markers.

Moreover, in the breaking-down of chronology, different ways of cohering and mapping knowledge are emphasised. For instance, a final-year module might investigate the thematic topic of the relations between literature and science from 1818, the year in which *Frankenstein* was published, to the present. Such a module would cut across periods and movements: it would locate Victorianism within 'a long nineteenth century', and it could embrace postmodernity, and thus might include texts such as Michael Crichton's *Jurassic Park*, and Greg Bear's neo-Darwinian techno-thrillers. Such a module could include Victorian texts such as Tennyson's *In Memoriam* (1850), H. G. Wells's *The Time Machine* (1895) and George Eliot's novella *The Lifted Veil* (1860). George Eliot has, for generations of English students, probably more often been encountered in period-based courses on Victorian literature, through lectures and seminars on *Middlemarch* (1870), in which her status as novelist-as-moralist is stressed. *The*

Lifted Veil provides a very explicit sense of George Eliot's interest in Romantic and mid-nineteenth-century science, which indicates the ways in which Eliot's moralism was inextricably linked to her reading of science. This, in turn, can provide a new way of reading *Middlemarch* that explores its complex engagement with science in, and sciences of, nineteenth-century society. The main point to stress here is the sense of intellectual excitement that can follow from a module that makes connections, often surprising ones, between literature and science in different historical contexts. Of course, no one is making the reductive claim that to read *Middlemarch* is 'the same as' to read Greg Bear's techno-thriller *Darwin's Radio* (1999). However, it is possible to think comparatively about these novels, and to think critically about how writers from different cultural moments, having at their disposal different scientific discourses, and different relationships to audiences and literary conventions, have used narrative to explore questions of heredity, gender and the role of scientific knowledge in society.

Technically, self-contained modules, in requiring that a certain number of aims and objectives are realised through teaching, learning and assessment in the course of study, are situated in a programme according to level, and the anticipated rate of skill acquisition (the skills required to make connections between literature and science of the kind outlined above are quite advanced). It should be noted here that while many programmes distinguish between different levels, some programmes only make a distinction between an introductory level and a more advanced level (it is normally only at the latter level that grades start counting towards degree classifications). Under the latter schemes, students from different cohorts can find themselves in the same classes, though some modules and forms of assessment (such as a dissertation) may be unavailable until year three or four.

If there is now a great deal of flexibility in the way that knowledge is imparted, it would be wrong to imply that there is an unchecked free-for-all in the construction of English literature degree programmes. The quality of higher education is a national concern, and organisations are empowered to establish frameworks that institutions need to observe when devising or revising an English literature programme ('programme specifications'). These frameworks are established after consultation, and are therefore grounded in what institutions actually teach, and, as a consequence, what English lecturers value and hold to be important. But they are designed to ensure that students on any programme of English literature are given opportunities to study a broadly equivalent range of texts, periods and critical and theoretical themes, and to acquire a comparable portfolio of skills.

4.2 LITERARY THEORY

Modularity is, in the end, an institutional solution to organising, imparting and assessing the acquisition of knowledge. It has affected all subjects, not just English literature. Literary theory, on the other hand, has had a more profound and specific impact on breaking up the chronologically progressive period-based study of English literature at university, as well as a received sense of what literature comprises. Our outline of a module on literature and science may not 'foreground' theory, though it would probably require its students to read some writings by Michel Foucault, Jean-François Lyotard and Donna Haraway. Foregrounded or not, it suggests that literary theory has set in motion intellectual tendencies that have brought such modules into being. As we shall show, literary theory has done much to enhance a critical sense of literature's inter-relatedness, interdisciplinary possibilities and historicity. In the concept of 'historicity', we try to capture the very complex ways in which texts co-exist in multiple historical 'moments'; the concept questions a literary history based only on 'historical progress', or 'succession'. As Joe Moran has argued, 'one of the principal aims of theory is the questioning of interpretations of the world that are usually taken for granted' (Moran 2002: 83). To that extent, theory and literature are doing the same kinds of thing. Perhaps the main difference is that theory is inclined to cast its re-interpretations of the world in an abstruse intellectual discourse, while literature is more inclined to do so through language that blends cognitive and affective responses. The crucial point is to find ways of connecting these enterprises. For, as Moran continues, 'theory is concerned with big questions about the nature of reality, language, power, gender, sexuality, the body and the self' (Moran 2002: 83).

At the same time, theory represents, as we have said in Chapter 1, potentially the most alienating part of the transition to university. It need not be, and to help us to see why not, it is perhaps important to unpack some of the difficulties that have accumulated around what some may take theory to stand for. If you take a standard anthology of literary theory, then it may appear to consist of a roll call of difficult non-Anglo-Saxon names. It may include the writings of Ferdinand de Saussure, Roland Barthes, Louis Althusser, Jacques Derrida, Michel Foucault and Pierre Bourdieu. Mikhail Bakhtin, Julia Kristeva, Hélène Cixous, and Jean-François Lyotard may be encountered. Their writings attempt to articulate intellectual methods such as structural linguistics, or concepts derived from this method. Concepts that have become important to theory include intertextuality, ideological interpellation of the subject, deconstruction, power/knowledge, cultural capital, dialogism, *écriture féminine*, and the postmodern collapse of grand narratives. If you are already in half a mind to put this book down and apply for a place on a computer science course, then you need to remember that all disciplines in higher education expect an engagement that, conceptually and theoretically, goes beyond what you have studied at A level or on an access course. History – a discipline known for its attachment to tried and tested empirical methods – has increasingly come to recognise the importance of theoretical reflection in the context of higher education.

All of the above names have been used to develop a body of knowledge that has come to be known as 'literary theory', but 'literary theorist' is not a label that any of these writers and thinkers might have attached to themselves. However, the concepts that they have elaborated have encouraged a rethink of the nature of literature's relations to the world. For example, Althusser's notion of the ideological interpellation of the subject helps us to articulate the point that we made about the relationship between subjectivity and power in Chapter 1; Foucault's notion of power/knowledge is also implicit in the kind of point that we made there. Roland Barthes's theoretical reflections on intertextuality are helpful for making the kinds of links between literature and scientific discourses in the examples given above.

There is little doubt that there was, in the 1960s and 1970s, a moment of 'theory' in which a range of disciplines from the humanities re-ordered their relations to one another and rethought their interpretations of the world. That moment was centred on France, in particular. Many of those named above are French philosophers and intellectuals who sought to rethink the disciplines of linguistics, psychoanalysis, anthropology and politics. In rethinking these disciplines, they reworked some of the writings of major intellectual figures of the modern period, such as Karl Marx and Sigmund Freud. Their writings were gradually translated into English and integrated by British intellectuals and academics into new ways of studying already constituted subjects, such as literature. The issue here is really about how theory is taught and 'translated' between contexts, context being perhaps the most enduringly important point to grasp about all aspects of literary study. There was a time when the majority of courses or modules in literary theory attempted to reflect the importance of a canon of theoreticians by teaching the writings of these 'master' thinkers, and exploring their impact on understandings of literature. Such courses undoubtedly continue to be taught today, and this approach to theory certainly has the merit of providing students with a detailed understanding of the main emphases of, and differences between, a complex corpus of writings. However, it seems to us that the consensus in theory teaching has been moving in a rather different direction, that is away, in some respects, from what might be described as 'high' theory. It is important always to bear in mind that intellectual life and the formation of academic subjects is a dynamic matter. The theory that had to be taught twenty, or even ten, years ago, because it was so new, was different from the theory that is increasingly seen as relevant now. And this is precisely because 'theory' as it first became established has been assimilated into new contexts. In being so assimilated, it has encountered new problems, has led to new interpretations, and has even helped to shape new literary work.

4.2.1 'High' theory: structuralist Marxism

In order to explore these points, it will be helpful to think about how a frequently taught literary text might be understood through different ways of reading with theory. Of course, what follows cannot be exhaustive, but these different ways of reading are schematically representative of theory's different, and, according to our argument, transforming relationships to literature. The difference is based around whether, first, literary texts are used to illustrate a particular manifestation of 'high' theory. Or, second, whether forms of theoretical understanding and relations are constructed and interpreted through a literary text and its multiple intertexts and contexts. The literary text we shall use is Charles Dickens's Victorian novel *Great Expectations* (1860–1), and we can begin with its opening:

> My father's name being Pirrip, and my Christian name Philip, my infant tongue could make of both names nothing longer or more explicit than Pip. So I called myself Pip, and came to be called Pip.
>
> I give Pirrip as my father's name, on the authority of his tombstone and my sister – Mrs Joe Gargery, who married the blacksmith. As I never saw my father or my mother, and never saw any likenesses of either of them (for their days were long before the days of photographs), my first fancies regarding what they were like were unreasonably derived from their tombstones. The shape

of the letters on my father's grave gave me an odd idea that he was a square, stout, dark man, with curly black hair. From the character and turn of the inscription, '*Also Georgina Wife of the Above*,' I drew a childish conclusion that that my mother was freckled and sickly. To five little stone lozenges, each about a foot and a half long, which were arranged in a neat row beside their grave, and were sacred to the memory of five little brothers of mine – who gave up trying to get a living exceedingly early in that universal struggle – I am indebted for a belief I religiously entertained that they had all been born on their backs with their hands in their trousers-pockets, and had never taken them out in this state of existence.

Ours was the marsh country, down by the river, within, as the river wound, twenty miles of the sea. My first most vivid and broad impression of the identity of things, seems to me to have been gained on a memorable raw afternoon towards evening. At such a time I found out for certain, that this bleak place overgrown with nettles was the churchyard; and that Philip Pirrip, late of this parish, and also Georgina, wife of the above, were dead and buried; and that Alexander, Bartholomew, Abraham, Tobias, and Roger, infant children of the aforesaid, were also dead and buried; and that the dark flat wilderness beyond the churchyard, intersected with dykes and mounds and gates, with scattered cattle feeding on it, was the marshes; and that the low leaden line beyond, was the river; and that the distant savage lair from which the wind was rushing, was the sea; and that the small bundle of shivers growing afraid of it all and beginning to cry, was Pip.

'Hold your noise!' cried a terrible voice, as a man started up from among the graves at the side of the church porch, 'Keep still, you little devil, or I'll cut your throat!' (Dickens 1965: 35–6)

It is important to remember that literary theory is not fundamentally dissimilar from literary criticism, an activity that you will have practised with more or less facility and awareness before you arrived at university. Literary criticism and literary theory are commonly concerned with the interpretation of texts; what we wish to demonstrate in differentiating between them is a process of building up readings through 'layers' (a process that we shall say more about in our skills-based account of reading and assessment in Chapter 5). As a close reader of *Great Expectations*, a number of points might strike you. For instance, that this is a first-person narration that introduces us to the character of Philip Pirrip, or Pip, the orphaned hero of the novel. Pip the narrator is clearly older than the orphan child Pip that he remembers and represents here: photography was not a part of his childhood world, but it is a part of his adult world. Literary critical close reading would urge you to think about the style of Pip's narrative voice. In particular, it might note that what the infant Pip comically 'sees' – the childish imaginary image of his dead brothers with their hands in their pockets – is rendered in a more sophisticated and ironic register than that of which a child would be capable. Voice is important to this opening; the ironic voice contrasts with the 'terrible voice' that concludes this passage. This is clearly dramatic, issuing a threat of death that looks terrifying indeed in the face of so much infant mortality.

But if the reader is looking for a phrase that coheres and organises this beginning and makes it a narrative opening, then it is the sense that this is Pip's 'first most vivid and broad impression of the identity of things'. As the reader will go on to discover, Dickens's novel is very much about impressions of the identity of things, and how those impressions have to be interpreted and re-interpreted. As a young man, Pip is moved away from his modest 'marsh country' life with his sister and her husband, Joe Gargery the blacksmith, and to a life of wealth and prosperity in London. Pip assumes that his benefactor is Miss Havisham, an embittered wealthy old woman who seems to have 'great expectations' of the boy's future. In fact, in the novel's famed narrative reversal, his benefactor is revealed to be Abel Magwitch, a felon and possessor of the 'terrible voice' that once commanded the child Pip to 'keep still' and then steal food for him before he was recaptured and transported. Magwitch the convict now provides for Pip through the fortune he has made in the penal colony of Australia.

A 'high' theoretical reading suggested by the writings of the structuralist Marxist Louis Althusser might still take these initial observations as a starting point. Because Marxism is a materialist theory of social relations, a Marxist approach to the novel would, for instance, be keen to analyse the question of social class: it would note that the orphaned Pip begins life as the lowly charge of his sister and her blacksmith husband, Joe Gargery. It would also note that Pip's social climb leads him into a world in which he is viewed as a 'gentleman', a man who does not work with his hands, and who becomes alienated from Joe's world. It would comment on contradictory class attitudes and discriminations that the novel explores. Pip has been proud to depend on the wealth that he mistakenly thought to be the gift of the bourgeois Miss Havisham, but he feels repugnance for that wealth when the source is revealed to be the convict Magwitch. But a specifically structuralist Marxist reading would also seek to examine Dickens's novel at a higher level of abstraction, and to think about how it functions as 'literature'.

To explain this higher level of abstraction and its implications for literature, it is necessary to say something about structuralism. Structuralist theory originates in the early twentieth-century linguistics of Ferdinand de Saussure. Saussure's main argument was that language functioned because it exists 'synchronically' in the present, and is a structured, autonomous and arbitrary system of signification. Saussure also speculated that his insights into the 'semiotic', or sign-based, nature of linguistic structure would have important implications for the analysis of a whole range of social practices and the way in which they were theorised. A later generation of mainly French writers pursued this insight. One was Louis Althusser, of whom more in a moment. But Althusser's work was itself responding to the work of Jacques Lacan, who reread the psychoanalytic writings of Sigmund Freud from the perspective of structural linguistics. Lacan was particularly interested in the way in which the individual, or 'subject', was formed by linguistic structures ('the symbolic order') and pre-existing 'subject positions'. Thus, the person is not born fully differentiated from others and individualised: instead, complex processes of social identification, separation and division are enacted. Something of this process is narrated in the opening of *Great Expectations*. Pip comes to know himself as an individual through a network of kinship relations (father, mother, brothers), and the trauma and terror that accompanies his growing sense of individuality: 'the small bundle of shivers growing afraid of it all and beginning to cry, was Pip'.

Althusser's Marxist perspective is set out in an influential chapter from his work *Lenin and Philosophy* (1971) entitled 'Ideology and Ideological State Apparatuses'. Althusser's theory sought to extend Lacan's theory of identity formation by examining the role that it played in sustaining and reproducing capitalist relations of production. For Althusser, these exploitative relations of production constitute the hard, material structures of social life. However, human subjects enter into 'imaginary' ways of relating to this material exploitation, and (mis)recognise the way in which they are placed within it (seemingly because humans find it difficult to bear too much reality). Subjects enter into these imaginary relations and are constituted as subjects because they are 'hailed', or 'interpellated'. If we look back at the opening of *Great Expectations*, we see that the act of 'naming' and being called a name is important. Pip thinks that he has named himself, and that others then call him by his name. However, what seems to be an act of original naming is in fact Pip occupying a pre-existing subject position, based on a corruption of his father's name, inscribed authoritatively on the gravestone that he has read. The name of the Father and the explicit allusion to Pip's 'Christian name' draw our attention to the authoritative systems for fixing identity that inscribe subjects into a particular moral and social order. And a cruel and unforgiving social order it is: Pip's deceased little brothers 'gave up trying to get a living exceedingly early in that universal struggle'. Consequently, because most of his close relatives are dead, Pip can only enter into 'imaginary relations' with the names and inscriptions that call upon him to realise an identity.

Pip is a reader of signs, inscriptions, from which he builds imaginary constructions. His act reminds us that we are readers of *Great Expectations* as literature. But how does Althusser's theory account for literature? Althusser's theory argues that hailing or interpellation is taking place all the time, in that all texts hail and thus constitute individuals as subjects of ideology. For Althusser, the most historically powerful and pervasive texts of ideological interpellation were put in place by 'ideological state apparatuses' such as the Christian church. During the nineteenth century, the period in which *Great Expectations* was written and set, the church continued to be an ideological apparatus, but it was supported by the power of the printing press. In turn, print produced many homiletic texts that sought to constitute readers as dutiful, respectful, and hardworking subjects; a good example would be Samuel Smiles's famous work *Self-Help* (1859). Althusser's theory does not assume that texts such as *Great Expectations* and *Self-Help* have precisely the same relationship to systems of ideology. *Great Expectations* may draw upon the harsh ideological language of nineteenth-century social thought; remember that Pip's brothers 'gave up trying to get a living exceedingly early in that universal struggle' and that this is enunciated in the ironic voice of the adult narrator. This is an important detail because for Althusser, literary art might use the materials of ideology, and yet it is distinct from simple ideological constructions. Literary art, Althusser contended, remains distinct and peculiar because it contains within it an 'internal distance' which gives the reader a 'critical view' of ideology (see Althusser's 'Letter on Art' (1966), Eagleton and Milne 1996: 269–74). Put simply, the complexity of literary art enables us to 'see through' the distortions of ideology, and to expose its limitations. If Pip is 'hailed' and fixed initially by the name of his Father (law), then the narrative of the formation of his identity is made immediately more complex by the way in which he is hailed by the address of a criminal, one outside the law. ' "Hold your noise!" cried a terrible voice, as a man started up from among the graves at the side of the church porch, "Keep still, you little devil, or I'll cut your throat!" ' And yet, as the narrative progresses, it becomes clear from Magwitch's story that a character can transgress the criminal law, but still live within a code of moral generosity.

It would be possible to extend this reading to explore the complex and contradictory ways in which Pip's identity is constructed and tested. The underlying assumption that motivates this kind of theoretical reading is that an enriched understanding of the ideological languages that Dickens's novel reworks to become 'literature' can be grasped by Althusser's theory, hence the prominence our reading has attached to questions of interpellation and 'hailing'. This high theoretical, abstract reading may be one that you are expected to undertake specifically in a course on literary theory, where a working knowledge of the theory and its application to the text is the aim of the class. You might be encouraged to make connections between Althusser and Dickens in the context of group work, or in the context of a seminar discussion that asks you to read the opening of *Great Expectations* alongside a selection of Althusser's writings on art and ideology. However, there are other ways of theorising Dickens's *Great Expectations* that invite a different kind of engagement, based on a different kind of theoretical focus or awareness.

4.2.2 Feminist, postcolonial and New Historicist perspectives

Literary theory is characterised by argument, debate and principled but conflicting interpretations that prioritise different details from the same text. For an influential critic such as Gerald Graff, these principled conflicts have become an important aspect of a literary education in a culturally plural world in which ethical engagement becomes more, not less, important. Althusser's structuralist Marxist starting point for the analysis of the ideology of subjectivity may not be an agreed starting point for every critic, given that different critics have different cultural and ethical priorities.

For instance, feminist literary theorists might argue that Althusser's theory is 'gender blind'. A feminist reading of *Great Expectations* might focus instead on women characters in the novel, pointing to the way in which Dickens builds Pip's narrative progress around certain 'types' of women: the cold manipulative narcissist (Estella), the embittered spinster (Miss Havisham), the 'un-maternal' carer (Mrs Joe), the 'maternal' carer (Biddy). A feminist perspective might note that all of these types remain fairly static – in the case of Mrs Joe, even violently silenced – and are seen from the exterior, while it is only Pip, the male narrator, who is endowed with interiority (his inner life being the subject of the story) and the drama of personal development over time. Feminist critics might argue that language in general, and literary language in particular, privileges masculine or even patriarchal points of view. The point that feminist theory strives to make visible is that representation is always marked by the codes and discriminations of an ideology which is gendered, and that these normally privilege masculinity, and silence or de-value femininity.

For other critics, Althusserian, and indeed feminist, theory might seem to be too Euro-centric (centred upon Western Europe). These theorists and critics might observe that class and gender relations in advanced capitalist social formations are particularly refined in, but peculiar to, Western Europe. They might go on to observe that other patterns of social organisation, exploitation and injustice might require a different kind of analysis in parts of the world that have been shaped by the experience of colonialism, and that these patterns could be interpreted in the literature about that colonised world. This would be the perspective of postcolonial theory. Edward Said has been one of the most influential voices in the formation of postcolonial literary theory since the publication of *Orientalism* (1978). In that work, Said argued that the production of English (and Western European) literature is intimately related to the structures of Western imperialism, and the cultural discriminations that it employs to support that enterprise (the occident as 'centre', the orient as 'other'). Said's *Orientalism* is a good example of the way in which theory is less about legislating from an authoritative position, and more about argument and debate. As Robert Young has recently argued, 'postcolonial studies has actually defined itself as an academic discipline through the range of objections, reworkings and counter-arguments that have been marshalled in such variety against Said's work' (Young 2001: 384). Postcolonial literary studies have in this sense been created by theoretical argument. Postcolonial literary study has indeed become a field of English literary studies in its own right, and many programmes now offer modules in postcolonial literature.

But the impact of postcolonial theory has been wider still. In Said's more recent work, *Culture and Imperialism* (1993), he argues that readers need to be alert to the processes of colonisation, and resistance to colonisation, that have characterised the experience of the modern world. For Said, this means rereading works of narrative literature to draw out the history of colonialism that is embedded in them, even in, for instance, your 'survey' module in Victorian literature. For instance, in Dickens's *Great Expectations*, the narrative drama and reversal depends upon Australia's original colonial function, as a penal settlement to which Magwitch had been sent without the right of return. Said argues that narrative is central to the relationship between imperialism and culture for 'nations are narrations. The power to narrate, or to block other narratives from forming and emerging, is very important to culture and imperialism' (Said 1993: xiii).

We can conclude by focusing on the postcolonial legacy of Dickens's *Great Expectations* while building on Said's point about national narratives forming, emerging, and re-forming, to illustrate the way in which 'theory' and literature are mutually imbricated and engaged in a kind of dialogue with one another. In 1997 the Australian novelist Peter Carey published a novel entitled *Jack Maggs*. The novel re-narrates the *Great Expectations* story, though this time not from Pip's perspective, but from the perspective of the convicted and transported felon who returns: the eponymous Jack Maggs. Maggs returns illegally from Australia and has to reconstruct his relationship to 'English things' through memory and story-telling. In shifting the narrative perspective in the direction of the convict, Carey suggests that national identity is a complex, layered phenomenon (much like our account of reading and textuality). In narrating this complexity, Carey rearranges the relationships that were central to Dickens's original fiction. He makes Dickens into a fictional character, the novelist Tobias Oates, who mesmerises Maggs and appropriates his convict story, turning it into a fiction.

This parallels Carey's practice, and the writer observes in a note at the beginning of his novel that 'the author admits to having once or twice stretched history to suit his own fictional ends'. *Jack Maggs* is a good illustration of the way in which contemporary fiction is self-reflexive about the practice of narration. In turn this can be linked to a broader theoretical tendency that explores the way in which the boundaries between fiction and history have become increasingly blurred. This blurring has been explored intellectually in a variety of theoretical movements, one of which is known as the New Historicism. The New Historicism begins from the observation that historical writing has within it elements of fiction, and that fictional writing has within it knowledges, or discourses, that effect and transact forms of power in the world. Accordingly, New Historicism begins from the argument that forms of knowledge are historically relative and above all 'made' – or fictionalised – by the culture in which they are embedded. Thus, the New Historicism investigates the relationships between forms of culturally 'permitted' fiction, such as drama, poetry and the novel, and forms of knowledge, including marginalised and so-called 'pseudo sciences'. In addition to its postcolonial reference points, *Jack Maggs* is a piece of contemporary fiction that explores this relationship, given the attention that it devotes to mesmerism, a science that, from the perspective of the present-day 'hard sciences' is dismissed as 'quackery', but which was important in the nineteenth century for the complex tapestry of 'power/knowledge' relations in which it was embedded. The point to grasp here is not that 'theory' stands over Carey's novel occupying some kind of high, explanatory all-seeing perspective on its meaning. Rather, 'theories' – from the intellectual landscape of the past, of nationality, of identity, of the relation between the 'fictional' and the 'real' – comprise a 'climate of discourse' within which contemporary literature and its intertextualities are being shaped. To be aware of literary theory is, consequently, to be culturally literate in new, exciting and highly relevant ways.

PART II
Study Skills in English Literature

5 READING

5.1 METHODICAL READING IN LAYERS

Reading is essential to every degree course. In a subject such as English literature, reading is at the very heart of the subject; your ability as a reader will often be the object of assessment, or the skill you will be called upon to demonstrate in essays, oral presentations and so on. This section will focus on what to expect from the way in which a degree course in English literature might attempt to develop your reading; and how you in turn should seek to develop your own reading skills independently, in tandem with the course.

In a discipline such as English language, although students will be encouraged to read widely, it is possible that a course of lectures will follow a set textbook. This is much less likely to be the case in the study of English literature, where it is more helpful to think about reading as a layered process of learning embracing many different texts. We saw in Chapter 4 how the impact of theory on the teaching of English literature has emphasised a relational view towards texts. Such a view needs to be carried through to the layered approach to reading that you will find it helpful to practise during study. In establishing these layers, you should recall the distinction between primary and secondary texts. Most courses will expect you to purchase your own copy of the primary text, though there may be back-up copies in your institution's library in case of emergencies. Your library will certainly be the main source of secondary texts, or criticism, literary history and theory. Libraries vary enormously in terms of layout, searching facilities, and styles of service: you should take advantage of any induction classes or tours of your library's facilities as early into your course as possible. One thing you can be sure of is that, on an English literature course, you will be one of many readers, often in search of the same volumes for reading towards the same topic. Of course, it is important to be well organised in your search for materials, being first in the queue where possible. But co-operation with other students and users over distribution and lending is as important a principle, not least because you won't always be able to be first in the queue.

Even though it is important to go searching in and borrowing from the library, the first layer of reading to establish in your approach to study involves the primary text. That is, the poem, dramatic text or narrative that you are to prepare for assessment (which may be for a seminar presentation, a 2,000-word essay, or even a dissertation). It is important that, as an increasingly independent learner, you adopt an active role towards the reading of this text. It is quite possible that, as a first-year student, you will find the reading that you have been set challenging, and not immediately accessible. This may be because the genre in which the work is composed is not familiar to you: for example, students often confide in their tutors that they find poetry difficult. The point is to find ways of meeting the challenge and not to feel defeated by it; try to adopt a methodical approach to your reading.

5.1.1 First layer: working on a primary text: Coleridge's 'Fears in Solitude'

For example, you have been asked to read Coleridge's poem entitled 'Fears in Solitude', situating its poetic and thematic features in context. Before reading the poem, consider its title closely: 'Fears in Solitude, written in April 1798, during the alarm of an invasion'. There are a number of key words in the extended title: solitude, fear, alarm, invasion. 'Solitude' provides some sense of the particular human state that the poem addresses: being on one's own, intensely aware of one's individuality. 'Fear' and 'alarm' suggest senses of deep anxiety, and 'invasion' indicates the source of that anxiety. The date, 1798, is also significant: the French Revolution had been in progress since 1789, and Britain was threatened by invasion from Napoleon's military forces (an abortive invasion attempt had been mounted on the Pembrokeshire coast in 1797). You can see that even in this preliminary act of reading, we are beginning to think about context, which is not something that is external to the poem and inert, a 'bolt-on' extra. Instead, the title is inviting us to think about context as a condition of reading the poem.

Now read the poem, using the key words from the title to organise your preliminary account of the poem's significance. You might consider reading the poem aloud; this will help you identify more readily particular sound qualities that are helping to construct and consolidate the meaning of the poem. For instance, in the opening lines, as we are introduced to a scene of great natural beauty, we are told that the 'swelling slope', below which the all-important 'small and silent dell' is situated, 'hath a gay and gorgeous covering on, / All golden with the never-bloomless furze' (Richards 1977: 137–44, ll. 4–6). This is not a strongly alliterative poem, but the emphasis on gay/gorgeous/golden suggests a site of abundant growth and activity. This contrasts with the 'green and silent spot', or 'quiet spirit-healing nook' (l. 12), the place in which solitude and a meditative attitude can best be experienced, and 'Religious meanings in the forms of Nature' divined (l. 24).

The opposition between noise and silence is very important to the poem. As the meditative, solitary speaker contemplates the future from the silent dell, what he imagines is the terrible noise of invasion and warfare: 'the thunder and the shout, / And all the crash of onset; fear and rage, / . . . Carnage and groans beneath this blessed sun!' (ll. 37–40). If poetry sometimes seems a daunting form of discourse because it will not yield its meaning without some difficulty, then that is the point. Usually, poetry strives to place distance between its own eloquence and heightened awareness of language, and what it constructs as the mere chaos of 'noise'. If warfare represents one very extreme example of this chaotic noise in 'Fears in Solitude', then 'ordinary speech' also carries its dangers:

> Meanwhile, at home,
> All individual dignity and power
> Engulfed in Courts, Committees, Institutions,
> Associations and Societies,
> A vain, speech-mouthing, speech-reporting Guild,
> One Benefit-Club for mutual flattery.
>
> (ll. 53–8)

According to the poem, the kind of routine and mechanical speech associated with these collective bodies and institutions actually strips the individual of dignity and power, a very serious matter given the value that the poem attaches to individuality and solitude. By contrast, the eloquence that the poem attains in addressing a national crisis is a testimony to what can be achieved by reflecting on the ills of society, both abroad and at home, from a position of solitude that is in touch with the divine power of nature:

> O native Britain! O my Mother Isle!
> How shouldst thou prove aught else but dear and holy
> To me, who from thy lakes and mountain-hills,
> Thy clouds, thy quiet dales, thy rocks and seas,
> Have drunk in all my intellectual life,
> All sweet sensations, all ennobling thoughts,
> All adoration of the God in nature.
>
> (ll. 182–8)

'Fears in Solitude' is a long poem, and the point here is not to provide a line-by-line reading of the entire work. Indeed, when reading, you do not have to note details in every single line, especially if you cannot see a point to the details that have been noted; the really important details are those that you can build into larger structures of significance and meaning. In practice – and going back to our advice about reading in layers – you will probably only be able to build up these larger structures of meaning upon reading the poem two or three times.

5.1.2 Adding layers: secondary reading

Let us build further on the process of reading in layers: you will, initially, have been preparing 'Fears in Solitude' by reading the text itself. But you have also been collecting secondary texts from the library, and these should be read so as to add layers of significance to the poem. These might include literary historical works on the significance of the Romantic movement in literature; literary critical works evaluating Coleridge as a poet; and accounts of the broader social, political and intellectual contexts that were shaping Coleridge's response to his time. Beginning to read a work of literary criticism or scholarship can appear daunting. However, you can adopt an intelligently selective approach to such reading.

It is essential to read your primary texts from beginning to end; reading only half of 'Fears in Solitude' will not make you a very authoritative or reliable reader. With secondary texts, your reading can and should be more focused on meeting the needs of a particular kind of enquiry. For instance, in reading 'Fears in Solitude', you will have established how important the idea of 'nature' is to Coleridge. Thus, when reading the literary historical work on the significance of the Romantic movement in literature, look to see if the book has a chapter devoted to 'nature', or use the index to guide your reading in a search for discussions of this topic. For example, you might look at R. L. Brett's 1971 volume *S. T. Coleridge* in the series *Writers and their Background*. 'Nature' in the index would take you to the opening paragraph of A. R. Jones's chapter, and this will warn you against taking Coleridge's representations of nature as naive descriptions of landscape. Indeed, this kind of insight might lead you to look closely at Ian Wylie's book, *Young Coleridge and the Philosophers of Nature* (1988). This will indicate in more detail the ways in which Coleridge's concerns with nature were part of the politics and intellectual fabric of his age.

When reading Coleridge's poem, you also established the way in which the banality of public political discourse emerges as a theme of the poem. If you were to read Nicholas Roe's

Wordsworth and Coleridge: The Radical Years (1988), you
would find that Roe's study is focused on the relationship
between Coleridge's writing and the social and political contexts of the 1790s. It would provide you with contextual
information on the role of debating societies as sites of radical
political argument in a Britain responding to the revolutionary
upheavals on the continent. It would also indicate the extent to
which the youthful Coleridge was himself a participant in this
radical culture. You might ask yourself how 'Fears in Solitude'
responds to these formations and institutions, and thus adopt
an ideological stance towards the validity of political activism.
Roe's book actually concludes with a reading of 'Fears in
Solitude'. It becomes clear from this reading, considerably
enriched by the detailed context that Roe establishes, that
some of the simple oppositions between 'nature' and 'public
discourse' that our first reading identified are not quite adequate. Guided in our reading by Roe, 'Fears in Solitude'
becomes more complex and contradictory. Reading in layers
to uncover dimensions of significance in the poem thus enables
you to assemble a multi-faceted awareness of context that
embraces the intellectual history of Romanticism as well as a
sense of the political situation that the poem both responded to
and, however uncertainly, sought to reshape.

Of course we read secondary works of literary criticism for
information. A work accounting for Coleridge as a poet can
inform us that 'Fears in Solitude' is a poem that can be
grouped into a series of Coleridge's works that have become
known as 'the Conversation Poems' (because they dramatise a
mind in conversation with itself, so to speak). However, it
would be misplaced to think that this kind of reading is simply
about acquiring information. Secondary texts are often referred to as 'sources': when nineteenth-century explorers went
in search of the 'source' of this or that river, the search
required a gradually acquired knowledge of territory and
intelligent mapping. Your reading of secondary sources should
involve similar activities. Even though you may be reading a
work of criticism selectively, you should also be reading it
actively. You should be asking yourself: what is this critic's

overall argument? What case, angle, or thesis is he or she attempting to advance about Coleridge, or nature in the Romantic period, or the place of poetry in political debate during the 1790s? The kind of thesis that the author is seeking to advance will have implications for the 'information' that the source will yield for you.

Students often seem to be reluctant to use articles in learned journals as sources of reading; 'learned journals' can sound intimidating and they can often be stored in what seems like the most inaccessible and mysterious part of the library. However, make the effort to become familiar and comfortable with gaining access to literature journals and periodicals. Due to their brevity, journal articles will often contain a focused discussion of the author, work, theoretical topic or contextual issue that you are reading around. To be accepted for publication in a journal will usually mean that the essay has a clear and well-articulated thesis that breaks new and original ground in making its case. Of course, when you are confronted by a journal that has been publishing for two, three decades – or longer – then there is a real issue regarding how to find relevant articles. Again, don't be put off, and above all, don't sit in that mysterious bit of the library flicking through number after number, hoping that something on 'Fears in Solitude' will 'turn up'. Instead, identify relevant articles via electronic databases, such as First Search, which should be your first port of call before visiting the location of the journals. For instance, use of this resource would indicate that Peter Larkin published an article entitled ' "Fears in Solitude": reading (from) the Dell' in a journal entitled *The Wordsworth Circle* 22: 1 (Winter 1991), 11–14. Before finally going in search of *The Wordsworth Circle*, check your library OPAC for those journals to which your library subscribes: many more journals are published than your library could reasonably hope to stock (for more on this, see Chapter 10).

When you are reading secondary sources, you should be looking to map a territory or, as academics call it, a field. For this reason it is very important to take accurate records of all the sources or 'landmarks' in the field that you have consulted during the course of your reading. If it is a book, then note the author, the title of the work, and any sub-title; its place of publication (for instance, London, New York, Cambridge, Edinburgh), the name of the publisher (for example, Edinburgh University Press), and finally the date of publication. If it is an essay in a journal, make a note of the author, the title of the essay, the title of the journal, and the year and issue number that the article is contained in. For instance, as in the example of the article from *The Wordsworth Circle*, you should record that Peter Larkin's article appeared in volume 22, issue number 1, published in the year of 1991, between the pages of 11–14 (for more detail on this, see Chapter 10).

6 GETTING THE MOST FROM LECTURES

Lectures are probably the most alien form of teaching that a new student on an English literature course will encounter. The experience of sixth-form teaching, or an access course, will probably be good preparation for tutorial or seminar teaching based on a relatively intimate, interactive discussion group. However, on first acquaintance a lecture will be more reminiscent of a school assembly. You are likely to be gathered with between 100 and 200 people (or more, most of whom will have the cold that you will soon catch), depending on the size of the programme to which you have been admitted. You will be addressed, normally for about fifty minutes, by a lecturer who may appear to be distant and remote, and who, spatially, may actually be distant and remote from you: university and college lecture theatres are large venues.

Why is English literature still taught, in part, via the lecture? It could be claimed that it justifies the official title by which teachers in higher education are named: they are, after all, lecturers, so it seems only right that they should lecture. 'Lecture' is an archaic term that, as *OED* informs us, was being used to describe authoritative learned addresses in English universities as early as the sixteenth century. It would be a mistake, however, to think that present-day lecturers are mindlessly clinging to tradition: for many teachers in higher education, lecturing is not their preferred mode of teaching, and discussion-based teaching tends to be more satisfying for everybody involved. English literature continues to be taught in this way in part because the lecture remains an efficient way of delivering a common body of information to substantial numbers of students, given that English programmes continue to recruit large numbers of well-qualified students.

So there is still a place for the lecture, not least because lecturers have in recent years sought to make it a lot less like the experience described above, transforming it instead into a more interactive form of learning. Lectures need not induce passivity. Do not be surprised if in the course of a lecture, your lecturer sets the whole group a task: for instance, think of three things that a literary critic does, or think of three things that are characteristic of narrative. The lecturer may then ask you to work with the person next to you in formulating a response to this task. The lecturer will probably recognise the impracticality of seeking feedback from everybody, so you may not be required to say anything in this large public forum: the main point of the exercise is to reinvigorate your engagement towards the topic of the lecture. That said, you should also feel entirely comfortable with approaching lecturers after lectures or asking questions within the lecture itself; it may be you need something repeating or clarifying or want to follow something up. Be proactive about making the lecture situation work for you; tutors will invariably appreciate your input and interest.

Also, many lecturers try, wherever possible, to use visual aids and information technology to engage attention. Such aids range from the overhead projector, to the sophistication of Powerpoint, and finally the humble but no less useful handout, which enables you to take a record of the lecture away with you. It is worth pausing for a moment to reflect on lecture handouts and how to use them. As lecturers, we notice when students ask to collect handouts on behalf of friends who have chosen not to attend. In truth, however, most lecture handouts need the context of the lecture to make them meaningful; they are a support to the lecture, not a substitute for it. Handouts will often contain quotations from the text that comprises the subject of the lecture; the aim in providing them is to prevent you from having to scramble around in that text (you may have a different edition from your lecturer). So don't just rely on these quotes when you come to write an essay or assignment. Use the handouts as models or templates for how to make quotes work for you and how to investigate and interrogate them. But try to ensure that you source exemplifying quotes of your own to supplement those discussed in lectures.

In stressing the importance of your independent involvement in the learning process initiated by lectures, you will clearly want to keep your own record of the lecture in the form of notes. This can become a source of anxiety, especially when you first begin your course, and the lecture feels new and perhaps alienating. How much should you record? Everything the lecturer says? Even those off-the-cuff remarks where he or she departs from a prepared script, and you are still trying to scribble down the previous point? This is where you need to become an active as opposed to a passive presence at the lecture, even when your lecturer is simply lecturing without setting interactive tasks.

The first thing you need to be is prepared. Check well in advance to see what the lecture is about. If it is about Salman Rushdie's *Midnight's Children*, then make sure you have read the novel in advance of the lecture; if it is about postcolonialism, look at the entry on this topic in a dictionary of literary critical terms before you go to the lecture. In other words, try to construct your own schema or frame of reference before the lecturer even begins to speak, for then you will be able to assimilate the lecture to knowledge that you are beginning to acquire for yourself. The worst thing that you can assume, especially in a subject such as English literature, is that a lecturer is there to present to you 'the last word' on a topic that can be transferred seamlessly into your own essays or exam answers. No matter the panache with which the lecture may be delivered, no matter that your lecturer speaks with authority and confidence, lectures can only ever be selective and schematic performances of a given topic. Thus, lectures on the innovative nature of Romantic poetry, the question of the rise of the novel, or critical arguments about *Hamlet* will draw on extensive bodies of primary and secondary reading; in fifty minutes, no lecturer could do justice to the nuances and complexities surrounding these topics. What he or she can and will do is to provide you with a model for critically engaging with these debates: the modes of reading, claims and counter-claims, arguments and counter-arguments that one needs to consider before commenting on them meaningfully. Lectures do provide you with 'information', but that information is always organised in the form of arguments, rather than incontrovertible fact. The publication date of Henry Fielding's *Joseph Andrews* may be a fact, but that may not be the most significant point to grasp in a lecture that ponders that text's role in helping to bring the modern novel into being.

All of this should help you to devise a note-taking practice for lectures. Use and follow the handouts or the overhead transparencies that the lecturer is employing; they are there to provide you with a clear sense of structure. If you can take the handout away with you, there will be no need to repeat information that it has already set out. Take selective notes, and use the lecturer's main headings to work out what is really crucial, and what is more incidental. Spend a lot of time listening to and absorbing the lecturer's points, and try to write down summary accounts rather than verbatim transcripts of the words and phrases used. Consider developing personal shorthand skills in lecture notes (most easily achieved for authors' names and text titles, but also usable for establishing contextual markers: C17, C19 for centuries, FrRev (French Revolution), W.Qu (the Woman Question)). You will retain much more than you expect, especially if you have done some preparatory work on the topic. Don't fetishise lecture notes, but instead treat them as working documents that will take you forward to new intellectual leads and enquiries. Continue to work on them and build them up with your own reading: follow up references that the lecturer has included by finding the relevant criticism in the library. Finally, there are no prizes for keeping neat lecture notes, but at the same time be honest about how effective your note-taking practice is. If on looking at your notes three or four days after taking them – say, before you are about to go to a tutorial – you cannot understand what you have written, then you may need to spend some time writing up your notes in more reflective moments after the lecture.

A final point stressing the need for mutual tolerance! As lecturers, we encounter and happily accommodate many different learning styles practised by our students. This book offers tips for guidance: how you put it all together, and the alternatives with which you supplement the guidance will be down to you. As students, you will, similarly, encounter many different lecturing styles. Some lecturers will talk spontaneously off the cuff from a series of prompting key cards. Some use transparencies to structure the order of ideas and the information being put across. Others have a prepared script that they use to structure ideas. All are valid means and methods – they may provide you with some interesting models and alternatives for your own oral presentations. Remember how hard it can be to control material even in a five-minute presentation and this may help you to appreciate the work put into a fifty-minute lecture. Some students also assume that a prepared script means that they might as well have just read the tutor's notes and not bothered to attend. This is a false assumption. The script is a structure but the engagement with the audience on the day will have a vital impact on the ideas and how they are expressed or even challenged. Sometimes students say people on TV can speak without notes so why can't lecturers? Autocues are deceptive things.

7 HOW TO USE A TUTORIAL OR TEACHING SESSION

7.1 WHAT IS A TUTORIAL?

As in many instances in this book, the terminology may vary according to institution, but it is safe to say that many of your courses or modules on an English degree will entail a combination of lectures and tutorials and/or seminars and workshops; or, to put it another way, they will involve a mixture of large group teaching or instruction and small group sharing and dissemination of ideas.

The numbers that constitute a 'small group' will also vary; anything from eight to twelve students is common, and some universities also conduct supervisions in pairs or groups of three to four students. But the essential aims and objectives of all these teaching methods inhere across these different modes of learning: in smaller group tutorials or seminars, students can share ideas, present research, and debate and scrutinise ideas relating to the course. The dissemination of ideas comes not solely from the direction of the tutor (of course, this is not always the case in lectures either, though it is a predominantly more instructive mode, see pp. 75–6), but also derives from the very act of discussing ideas within a group setting.

For that reason, what you might do within a single tutorial or seminar will differ widely, sometimes from week to week. The duration of these sessions will also vary according to institution and group size, as well as what stage you are at in your studies. A reasonable expectation would be a session lasting between one and two hours. In a given session, you might be studying a specific text that you have prepared as a group – a play, poem or novel, for example – or you might be analysing a poem or a piece of film that you are reading or seeing for the first time. Alternatively, you might be participating in or listening to oral presentations, carrying out group work on a specific topic, or reporting back to the group on research you have carried out into a specific topic outside of the affixed tutorial time. You might be discussing material within the group as a whole, or within smaller sub-groups, or even pairs. Suffice to say, then, that tutorials, seminars and workshops, whatever the title of the particular mode of learning you are experiencing at any given time, are dynamic, fluid forms. That is part of the fun of learning situations at university.

These sessions are frequently also the area of a course or module in which students find it easiest to develop their own critical voices or opinions. Some lecture halls or formats can seem rather forbidding, but it is less nerve-wracking to venture an opinion in a workshop. For that reason, the study skills that you develop in approaching them will be a crucial part of your learning experience at university.

Tutorials and seminars are occasionally, but not always, part of your assessment programme. If your participation in and contribution to them is being formally assessed, then the criteria for this will be established with you by the lecturer or tutor at the start of the course. Simply speaking out a lot in seminars will not necessarily ensure a high assessment mark. Careful and thoughtful preparation and the ability to listen and take on board the ideas of others are a crucial part of the experience. If you think you are struggling with any aspects of tutorial work, try and seek guidance as soon as possible; lecturers' office or consultation hours are often the best means of obtaining this advice and guidance.

All aspects of degree courses are designed to allow you to develop and nurture your skills and tutorials and seminars are no exception. A student does not necessarily have innate tutorial skills: team-working, presentation skills and knowledge of how to prepare well are all abilities that you will be able to acquire as the weeks go on and your confidence in your abilities grows.

7.2 PREPARATION FOR TUTORIALS AND SEMINARS

Often on an English literature module or course you will be assigned set texts to prepare for specific seminars or tutorials. Part of your preparation for that teaching session will therefore be the reading and comprehension of that text, or, perhaps, the viewing of a film or, in a performance-based course, a particular production of a play on video, in advance of the session. One of the most important study skills to acquire as a literature undergraduate is a full understanding of what 'preparation' means. Simply reading a text from cover to cover or from start to finish does not constitute, by any means, adequate preparation for a seminar. You should also have begun the process of analysing that text: drawing out features which to you seem important, such as central themes or topics, of course, but also questions arising from the text's formal aspects. If your set text is a poem, you might, for example, makes some notes relating to the metre, rhythm or prosody (that is to say, its versification) of that poem. Try reading the poem aloud and see what strikes you: are particular aural aspects of the poem worth commenting on (sibilance or assonance, for example)? Are there strategies of repetition to observe? If you are studying a play, as well as noting what happens in each act or scene, you might want to record some observations about the dramaturgic structure of the text. Is it important in which act or at what stage of the play something happens? Is everything resolved in the final act? Are certain scenes placed alongside each other – juxtaposed – for a specific reason? Are there certain scenes worth looking at in detail because they offer examples of particular conventions (soliloquies or overhearing scenes, for example)? Make notes on all these observations so that when you are in the tutorial or seminar you don't suddenly go blank and forget all the hard work you have put in. These preparatory notes will give you the confidence to raise points for discussion and you can add to them, refine or nuance them, as the seminar or workshop progresses.

Frequently, preparation involves looking at material related to the set text as well as the primary text itself. Humanities subjects such as English literature have a lot of reading time built into the structure of the degree and you should make the most of the opportunities this provides. Course reading lists may well guide you as to what secondary material or criticism will aid you in unpacking the meanings and literary strategies of your focus text or film. You will not be able to read everything but pick out one or two books or articles that are of particular interest to you, go to the library and read up on them, make notes and, again, bring that information along to the seminar to share with fellow students. In the best learning situations, you will find other people have looked at different texts and you can swap information and points of interest.

Sometimes specific areas for your readings or specific secondary material to explore will be highlighted for your attention in advance of the session by the tutor or lecturer in the form of preparatory worksheets or preparatory questions assigned in a previous seminar. If you are given a worksheet of this kind, make the most of them since they will help to focus your reading and provide you with points of discussion within the seminar itself. If all the students have looked at related areas, it can really facilitate lively debate and avoid those awkward silences that we all know can be a problem in seminar discussions.

In other situations, however, you may simply be asked to prepare the set text for the following week. Often the structure of the course as a whole will give you clues as to how to approach the text. Ask yourself, for example, does the course or module have a specific aim, such as the study of the topic of money in nineteenth-century fiction or science and literature? If so, you already know what the main themes are that you will be looking for in the set texts. Sometimes lectures will also give you guidance or ideas that you want to follow up for yourself. Find your own intellectual pathway through the material so that you have something to say in seminars specific to you and the way you read and approach texts.

One of the most important skills to hone, then, is how to

make preparatory notes for tutorials or supervisions that really work for you. Develop strategies for approaching particular kinds of texts. There will be certain models that work for approaching a novel that will not work for approaching a play. Think early on in your studies about the conventions of particular genres and use these to structure your note-taking in the early stages of thinking about a text. If you are looking at a novel, think about the plot development but also the narrative strategies deployed for that purpose. If the novel has a first-person narrator, why not select two or three sample passages, in order to explore how the narrative voice functions in detail? It is a good rule when preparing texts for discussion to think about local issues as well as the overall structure or impact of the text. Pick out one or two passages of a novel and prepare them in real detail: pick out one or two specific scenes of a play and really unpack how they are operating. Think about all the things that are specific to a play. How would that scene be staged? Who is on stage at any given time? If they are on stage, are they speaking or silent? How do they speak? Do they share conspiratorial asides with the audience? How does that affect the scene? Generic conventions can be a wonderful springboard for thinking about what texts are doing that is special or even unique. Think about the rules and where texts adhere to them and then where they deviate or subvert them will become clearer. If you have a poem or a piece of dramatic poetry (such as Hamlet's 'To be or not to be' soliloquy, for example), find where the conventional English poetic line of the iambic pentameter is adhered to and then look at those lines where it is deviated from (for a working example of this, see pp. 13–14). Why does the poet want to draw your attention to those lines in particular? If the whole poem is very regular, why might order and regularity be the mood, atmosphere or tone the poet is striving for? How does this relate to themes or messages you have identified elsewhere in your notes as the central reading of the poem? Close readings of this nature can be really valuable to share with the group and to test against the ideas of others in a tutorial situation.

The central point here, then, is that preparation means a lot more than just 'reading the text through'. Time management (which we have discussed in another section in detail; see Chapter 8) comes into operation here. Structure the week in between seminars to allow time to read the text, and where possible to reread it. In the case of a poem, you might be able to read and reread it several times over the course of the week and you may well find that your views shift and alter as you do. Record these changes in your notes; these thought processes will be helpful to go back to if you are revising the text for an essay or examination (for more on revision techniques, see Chapter 11). Allow time to take sufficient notes and to brainstorm those areas you would really like to see discussed in a teaching session. Tutors will invariably appreciate this kind of input from students. If you have a worksheet or series of questions to prepare, allow time to do these adequately and also allow time to follow up your personal reading and note-taking with genuine forays into secondary material. In other words, pace your consideration of the text throughout the week or period of preparation you have – don't leave it all to the night before, thinking that somehow it will be more 'fresh' as a result.

7.3 ATTENDANCE AT TUTORIALS AND TEACHING SESSIONS

Attendance is a necessary element of your degree course and sometimes it is also a part of the formal assessment. Make sure you let tutors know if you are ill and are unable to attend. Make sure you also fulfil any formal requirements, such as the completion of self-certification forms that your university may require for the purpose of keeping records of attendance and absence. Ask for any preparatory sheets for the next week to be sent to you or collected by a fellow student on your behalf so that you don't find that you fall two weeks behind. Also make sure that you borrow notes or discuss what was covered in the session you missed with fellow students.

Tutorials and seminars are usually the venue in which

information about formal assessment procedures on a course or module will be provided – essay questions, exam preparation and so on. Make sure, therefore, that if you do miss a seminar you have not missed out on crucial information such as essay submission dates or the distribution of titles. Tutors will sometimes leave material for you to collect later in folders on their door or in your pigeonhole or in the school or departmental office. Get acquainted with the system and make sure you don't miss out on vital material.

Be proactive about using these occasions to raise any questions and concerns you might have. Having said this, also try to assess whether the questions you are asking are specific to you and therefore whether they might be better placed in a private consultation with the tutor during one of their office or consultation hours. Try to respect the purpose and function of a seminar and ask questions and raise issues accordingly. Ostensibly, seminars are spaces in which to discuss the assigned material and set texts, and more practical matters such as essay extensions or personal advice on using the library or setting out essays should be kept for consultation hours.

7.4 RELATIONSHIP BETWEEN LECTURES AND TUTORIALS

In the previous chapter, we discussed how to approach lectures and how to take notes in lecture situations. The relationship between lectures and tutorials is an important one to recognise. Once again, this will vary according to institutions – in some universities, lecture programmes are entirely separate from the tutorials, which are tied to particular courses, options or modules. In many institutions, however, lectures and tutorials are part of a linked programme, although the people who give your lectures will not necessarily be your tutors as well. Tutorials do provide a means of pursuing in detail, or following up, points or issues raised in lectures. You may frequently be asked at the start of a session what material or questions you covered in lectures on the set text. Courses have invariably been designed not to simply repeat material but to allow the tutorials to build on and nuance the points or contexts provided by the lecture. Bring your lecture notes along to tutorials as well since they may help you in raising related points. Do not be afraid to ask the tutor or fellow students to clarify or discuss points that confused you in the lecture or that you would simply like more time to discuss and explore. Be proactive about making the links and connections between the different elements of your modules. Lectures should not be something that exist in a space discrete from the preparation for and participation in seminars.

7.5 DISCUSSION IN TEACHING SESSIONS

Discussion is the central aspect of any seminar or tutorial. This discussion can, however, take a variety of forms. Sometimes you will discuss things as a whole group with people chipping in as and when they feel they have something to offer or when they want to take issue with a point or reading offered by someone else in the group. These discussions can be lively, but they should always be generous in spirit. Challenge other people's views by all means but do it in the spirit of debate not in an effort to win points. Be supportive when listening to and considering the views of others. It cannot be stressed enough that seminars are as much about obtaining listening and teamwork skills as the skill to speak up on issues yourself. Think about the group dynamic: engage with the group as a whole – don't just address your points to the tutor, for example – and try not to dominate discussions: let everyone have a say. Similarly, if you think members of the group are dominating the discussions to the detriment of yourself or others, raise this point with the tutor in a consultation hour and the problem can usually be addressed quietly and tactfully. It really helps to foster discussion both within seminars and outside the tutorial itself if you get to know the names and interests of your fellow students. If you have the time in your timetables, and a number of you are keen, why not follow up the seminar discussion over a coffee later in the day? Remember that you have much to learn from each other as students on degree courses.

As well as whole-group discussions, seminars will regularly be broken down into smaller group work: maybe in subgroups of three or four, or even in pairs. Hopefully, in this way, you will get to speak to and work with lots of different people in the group. This will help to widen and vary your views. Group work of this kind might seem rather nerve-wracking when you first start out and find you don't know anyone, but it is a great way to break down social and intellectual barriers and to get to know the group: so, take a deep breath and plunge in.

7.6 NOTE-TAKING IN TEACHING SESSIONS

As we have stressed elsewhere in this study skills section, many learning methods are very personal and subjective, and peoples' approaches do differ. Some students like, for example, to take lots of notes during a seminar or tutorial and will bring along a pad of paper and pens for the purpose of doing so. Others prefer to try and listen hard and then brainstorm the session after the event. Both methods have their advantages. Do bring writing materials along to sessions, however, since you will need them for recording group discussions to report back to the whole group or sometimes to make 'brainstorming lists' at the seminar leader's request. Do bring along your set texts as well since the tutor may wish to concentrate on particular poems or passages in the context of the tutorial. As with any teaching session, come prepared. Bring your text, preparatory notes and writing materials with which to record what you learn or start to think about in the course of the session itself. This will make the process of thinking about the tutorial or seminar afterwards much easier.

7.7 DELIVERING AND LISTENING TO ORAL PRESENTATIONS

Giving an oral presentation, sometimes on your own or in a pair or sub-group, will often be a part of a course and may or may not be assessed. The length of presentations varies, but they usually last for five to ten minutes. They are an important part of the skills training element of a degree and will help to give you confidence about discussing your ideas. Advice will be given on this element of your course and there are now books and videos available that guide you as to best practice – we have listed some of these under 'Further reading' at the back of this book. There are some easy rules to remember. The first is to think about your audience. You will have listened to presentations as well as giving them before. Think about what worked for you: be clear about your aims and objectives, develop a line of argument and make that clear to your audience. To achieve this you may find the aid of a whiteboard or an overhead transparency – if these pieces of equipment are available in the teaching room – helpful, or alternatively, you may wish to provide a handout. Time your talk carefully. The length of presentations has been considered in detail by the department and the tutor and to overrun is to fail one of the essential components of this element of the course. Practise at home in your bedroom or study with a clock, and even a mirror to make sure you are looking up from your notes and engaging with your audience. Try to speak from key cards or notes: don't write out the paper word for word (and certainly don't reproduce that on a handout for others – this is a sure-fire way to stop them listening to you). This will ensure that you sound more natural and engage with the audience.

Your response to the presentations of other students is also crucial. Listen, take notes, ask questions afterwards and en-gage with their ideas. Think about how you would like others to treat your work when you present it in this format. The thoughts of other students are just as, if not more, valid than those of the tutor in this respect. Don't assume that because the tutor ultimately marks your essays and exams that he or she is the only person you have to persuade in the room.

7.8 OTHER METHODS OF PARTICIPATING IN TEACHING SESSIONS

Sometimes presentations will be peer-assessed – assessed or graded by your fellow students – rather than tutor-assessed or moderated. This is a wonderful means of learning what you look for in a presentation and applying those same criteria to your own projects. Some courses will also deploy methods of peer-assessment for written assignments. Once again, regard these exercises as a means of testing your own classificatory standards and then use those established standards to measure and judge work you submit or prepare in future.

Occasionally students are asked to 'lead' seminars in a given week. This can be a really empowering exercise. Suddenly you can see what it takes to put together a teaching session and, hopefully, you'll come out with more respect for what your tutor is doing every week on your behalf. But you also have the freedom to pursue debate on areas of particular concern to you. Remember that the point of the exercise is not for you to talk yourself silly for the session but to facilitate and encourage the discussion of others on topics of interest. Try to structure the session: vary the elements from whole-group discussion to small-group work. Perhaps you could assign different topics to different sub-groups. Bring along additional material such as extracts from critical articles, or maybe visual aids that will stimulate discussion. Making demands on the other students in terms of preparation for 'your' session may well help you to clarify and confirm what you should be doing each week in preparation for other tutorials.

7.9 FOLLOWING UP ON TEACHING SESSIONS

Students often become highly proficient at preparing for and participating in tutorials, seminars or workshops. As the weeks and months progress, what is needed in terms of preparation for a session becomes clearer and strategies and methodologies form themselves as part of the everyday practice of the student. What is perhaps less common is for the same degree of care and concern to be exercised about following up on tutorials once they are over. There is something of a temptation to think that that the focus text has now been 'done' and dealt with and not to think about it again until assessed essays and exam revision come around. Best practice, however, will be to build into your structure of time management a space after tutorials in which to write up, reflect upon and sometimes pursue further points that were raised. That is where note-taking within the tutorial itself will prove useful: those notes will provide a focal point for these retrospective considerations. You may wish to go and see a tutor in an office hour to clarify or follow up on a point, and lecturers can often suggest ideas for further reading that will enable you to do so. If particular theoretical terms have arisen in discussion that are new to you, go and look them up in dictionaries or glossaries of critical terms and add those to your notes. And don't forget to keep thinking about each text in relation to any new text you might be preparing for a future seminar. Essays and exam questions will invariably ask you to make links or draw comparisons between texts and if you have approached your studies throughout a semester or term in this spirit or frame of mind this will seem second nature rather than a frightening prospect.

Try then not to think of tutorials as stand-alone events but as part of an overall structure in which your ideas and thinking – on the texts, on the course and on the discipline as a whole – will emerge in a developmental and evolutionary fashion. Make the connections, draw the links, and the whole process will seem much more exciting and rewarding as a result.

8 TIME MANAGEMENT

When science undergraduates get together with friends who are studying English literature, amazement can be expressed at the relatively light load of classes that the latter are required to attend. The scientist who is spending the best part of her working week in class and laboratory will compare herself to the English student who is spending between six to eight hours in lectures and tutorials, and conclude that English must be 'a doss'. The English student would be unwise to believe this.

English literature programmes do not consist of a light workload, even though their students are seldom required to spend long hours in the classroom. Whereas an A Level syllabus may have required you to acquire an in-depth knowledge of six to eight texts over a two-year period, you will probably be required to read at least this many texts for your first semester's work (normally twelve weeks) on an English degree. And tutors will consider this quite a light, introductory load, designed to 'pace' your working speed so that you are prepared for something more demanding again at level two. Thus, one of the major challenges that new students face is that of managing their independent learning time so as to get the best from the teaching time and assessment regime that is scheduled. You cannot, and should not, spend all your time out of the classroom or lecture-theatre working, as socialising is essential to a fulfilled life at university or college. But nor should you spend all of your time sitting in the coffee bar waiting for inspiration and friends to move you in the direction of the library.

Effective time management begins upon reckoning up what you have to achieve in a given period. Don't be afraid to make lists, not least because it can be satisfying to tick off tasks once they have been completed. In making your lists, note the goals

92

that have to be achieved in both the short term and the long term. For whilst the most intensive demands on your time will be made during periods of teaching, your commitment to your degree should be maintained even during vacation periods. Thinking in the short term, take the working week as time that has to be managed. Organise your independent work around the specific goals that have to be achieved. Thus, on Tuesday, you have a lecture on *A Midsummer Night's Dream*; on Thursday you have a seminar on the same text. You should have read the play by the Tuesday so that you can engage with the lecturer's arguments. You might perhaps pencil in a visit to the library on Wednesday to consult any criticism that the lecturer recommended, which might help you to prepare for the follow-up seminar. Reading a play should not take you very long; but bear in mind our comments (Chapter 5) about the need to read in 'layers', which includes more than one reading of the given play. And in most weeks, you will have more than one reading task to complete, as you may well be studying three or four modules simultaneously if you are studying a single-honours programme. Think realistically about your preparation and the time that it will require. Thus, if you have to read a novel for a lecture and a seminar, unless you are a very rapid reader, you should probably begin to read this text at least the week before you are expected to discuss it. If you are expected to read a long novel – say by Charles Dickens, or Herman Melville, George Eliot or Don DeLillo – then begin to read it three or four weeks before you are scheduled to talk about it. You will find that you will be expected to read and have an intelligent working knowledge of texts that will not always accord with your personal sense of good or enthralling literature, so don't shy away from setting yourself quite mechanical reading goals. Tell yourself that you will read and make notes from the next 100 pages in the next three hours.

It should be clear from the advice offered above that short-term time management and long-term time management are not mutually exclusive: in week four, you will have to begin the reading that has to be completed by week seven. Effective time management involves assessing the scale of the tasks that you are expected to undertake. You need to bear such scales and time-frames in mind when planning for assessments. You should begin them well in advance of the submission date in order to facilitate visits to the library, recalling reading material that may be out on loan, reading and thinking time, planning and writing time, and redrafting time. And don't forget to factor in writing up and printing time, if you are using word-processing facilities. Printers have a habit of breaking down with two hours to that essay deadline remaining. Time management involves expecting such things to happen by not leaving everything until the last possible moment. Ideally, you will have discovered the problem with the printer on completing your essay the day before the deadline, which will have enabled you to make alternative arrangements.

Time management will inevitably become more complex the further you progress with a degree in English literature, so this is a skill that you will have continually to reassess and refine. So much of effective time management depends on a realistic assessment of one's life situation. If you live a long way away from your university library, then don't plan to acquire your secondary reading on the assumption that you can 'pop in' to the library whenever the fancy takes you. Plan to visit the library after you attend your next class. Time management is an essential transferable skill that will be as relevant to you in your working life after graduation as it will be to success in your degree.

9 ASSESSMENT

As we have already observed, there is an integral relation between the reading you will undertake for tutorials and the way in which you will be assessed. For instance, it is possible that the programme on which you are studying may assess some of your tutorial performances. Chapter 7 on how to use a tutorial or teaching session provides advice about how to get the most from these learning experiences through active engagement in discussion. Clearly, you will be rewarded for being an active participant. However, if you are not a well-informed active participant, it is actually possible to do yourself damage. Tutors tend not to feel generous towards the student who opines forthrightly that 'I've not read the book, but from what I've heard it seems like a lot of nonsense.' The extent to which you have read in preparation for a tutorial, and can demonstrate your grasp on that reading in the course of discussion, will contribute significantly to success in this form of assessment.

Assessed oral presentations are of course much more obvious set-piece occasions. Again, advice on how to prepare for these and deliver them in the context of the tutorial, in which the presentation will be time limited and addressed to an audience of peers, can be found at page 89. However, it is important to be aware that these contextual factors will shape the aims and objectives of the assessment. The aims of the assessment will be to see how effectively you can establish grounds for a tutorial discussion of a given text within the stipulated time-frame (normally five or ten minutes). Clearly then, the extent to which you have come to know the text, and the critical issues that it raises, will be important. A good working knowledge of the text will enable you to draw the attention of other members of the group to salient passages of text. An awareness of the critical and interpretative issues that have been generated by the literary criticism of the text will enable you to present these to the group, and open up some potential lines of discussion. If you are required to work as part of a group, it will be important to establish an appropriate division of labour early on, to ensure that you don't all work on precisely the same aspect of the project. In this instance, your ability to work and plan as part of a team would be one of the objects of the assessment. Generally speaking, it can be said that in recent years lecturers in higher education have become much more aware of the need to vary the diet of assessment to which their students are exposed. Consequently, while the essay remains the most important form of assessment on most degrees in English literature, additional modes of assessment are being developed to cultivate skills that can be used in contexts that go beyond the study of literature.

9.1 ESSAYS

The word 'essay' derives from the French word meaning 'trial', or 'test'. This does not mean however that this form of writing has always been a quality-assured mode of assessment. Instead, the essay came about when writers 'tested' the authority of received wisdom and doctrine against their own experience of living in and reflecting on a complex and changing world. The French Renaissance writer Michel de Montaigne produced a captivating example of such writings in his appropriately titled *Essais*. A successful example of the literary-critical essay still has something in common with its early generic origins. By this, we mean that the essay you will write ought still to be a 'test' of received wisdom and authority. We can illustrate this by getting inside standard features of the essay question. These often consist of a quotation from a critic – for instance, Henry James's judgement of George Eliot's *Middlemarch*: 'a treasure house of detail but an indifferent whole' – followed by a question, such as 'To what extent is James's judgement of Eliot's novel a valid one?' The question makes the quotation from James into a proposition, or authoritative pronouncement, with which your essay is invited either to agree or disagree. Of course, implicit in the act of agreeing or disagreeing with James is your critical work in closely reading Eliot's novel, as well as the critical evaluations of the novel of which James's judgement is just one. In order to write adequately on such a topic, you would need to have read quite widely, and with a sense of purpose, by asking yourself such questions as 'What did James consider to be a good novel, and why did *Middlemarch* not conform to that standard?' You could answer this by reading the review of *Middlemarch* in which James opined this view. And 'Why, from the evidence of her narrative voice, might Eliot have chosen to employ the very complex method of plotting and narration that produces so much detail in the novel? What did this detail say about history, provincial life and the woman question that James found difficult to appreciate?' An essay is thus a balance between, on the one hand, an engagement with the authority of received authority, and, on the other, one's own testing or trial of that authority.

An essay does remain a 'test' in the more conventional sense as well: it is possible to do either well or badly. Clearly, deficiencies in writing skills can be a factor here, but we shall have more to say about that at page 117. On the whole, students tend to perform badly in essay writing because they fail to argue their points effectively, either by not having enough evidence from the text and secondary reading, or by being opinionated and not much else. In testing the authority of existing criticism, it is important to cast your case in the form of an argument. This is the difference between saying 'I don't agree with X', and 'I don't agree with X because of Y, and so it follows from that we value Z in significantly different ways.' Tutors genuinely want to hear your views on a topic, but there are – as in most walks of life – ways of expressing them that will help to bring about greater levels of success. The same may be said of furnishing an essay with a proper system of referencing and citation. Insistence on this may appear to be mindless pedantry that gets in the way of the genuine expression of your views and convictions about a topic, and to be marked down for not including one a seeming insult. However, if we accept that literary writings and the published criticism that addresses them are 'landmarks' in a field, then an essay which references the material it has used to make its claims becomes something of a landmark in its own right. A properly referenced essay could also, more practically, guide another person who sought to use the essay as a source of reference (which is why bibliographies and notes are such useful things). Accurate use of quotation and citation could also help to forestall any suspicion of plagiarism, a topic with which we will deal at pages 115–16. Finally, essays can go wrong because they fail to stay relevant to the topic set. Accordingly, it is important to think through in advance what you want to argue, and to plan an argument that keeps the topic in view. This isn't to say that you will not, as you write, find yourself having little disagreements with, or uncertainties about, your proposed argument. Writing is only exciting and intellectually real when it is not completely predictable. However, one is not equipped to meet these challenges if one is writing completely aimlessly.

9.2 OTHER KINDS OF WRITING: BOOK REVIEWS, ANTHOLOGY CONSTRUCTION

Essays are not the only kind of written assessment that you may be asked to undertake. You may, for instance, be asked to write a book review, or even to select poetry for an anthology and then to write the introduction to your selection. The aim here will be to familiarise you with some of the writing techniques that are regularly used in sustaining literary criticism and theorising as practices. Preparing an anthology can be a valuable exercise: it requires you to think about how selections are made from the vast array of writings that are available, and thus how canons are formed. Writing an introduction to an anthology can lead you to insights into how one might address an imagined audience: will you be writing your introduction for specialists? Or will it be for a group of beginners? These are considerations that an academic essay may not always invite. In writing a book review, you ought, unless guided otherwise, to use book reviews that appear in periodicals and learned journals as a model (book reviews which appear in newspapers or magazines tend to address a general audience, and you should assume that your audience is an academic one). To review a work of literary criticism, literary history or theory should help you to appreciate the stages of research, thinking, planning and writing that accumulate to make an academic book. One can appreciate this while still aiming to be constructively critical of the argument that is being reviewed. In writing a book review, you should reflect on the nature of the argument that is being advanced: how has that argument helped you in advancing your understanding of the topic that the book addresses? In being constructively critical of a book, you must first have grasped its argument. Once you have done this, you can ask questions such as: what has the author included or excluded? What might the book have been able to say if it had adopted a different kind of literary critical or theoretical orientation? In many respects, book reviews are forms of writing that can be very helpful for preparing to write essays. They can be even more helpful for preparing to write the dissertation, which will probably be the most ambitious mode of assessment that you will be asked to address on an English literature degree.

9.3 DISSERTATIONS: FROM PROPOSAL TO SUPERVISION

In the course of your English literature degree you will write many essays, but probably only one dissertation or long essay. It is most likely that you will be asked to write a dissertation in your final year of study, but you will be prepared for this. Generally, programmes of study devote a great deal of thought to considerations of academic level and the challenges that students can reasonably expect to meet during their course of study. First-level modules will be aware that students will need to make a transition between A Level/Higher modes of study, and the level of first-year degree work. Accordingly, you may find a relatively light reading load on such modules. However, it is important not to be seduced into thinking that a lighter reading load equates to an easy ride (especially if you are combining English with another subject that, superficially, appears to place more 'demands' on your time). If you are addressing your studies properly, you will be adding layers of critical reading to the primary reading that you are working on and becoming an increasingly independent learner. At second-year level, you will find that the volume of primary reading is likely to increase in courses of various kinds. However, it will still be important to read widely around these texts and the themes and topics that frame them. If you have put down secure foundations by developing good study habits in your first year, you will find this transition easier to manage. It is important to try to develop yourself as a fairly widely read and independent learner by your second year, not least because this may be the point at which you are asked to formulate a dissertation topic.

The dissertation is normally conceived as an independent piece of research and writing. When formulating your dissertation topic, it is important to focus on something that interests you; after all, you will have to be motivated to work independently on the topic, and probably for a sizeable portion of the academic year (a semester, maybe more). So, if you are a science-fiction enthusiast, it is quite possible that you will be able to write a dissertation on science fiction so long as there is a tutor contributing to your programme who feels sufficiently knowledgeable to supervise it. Just one word of warning though: if you are an uncritical enthusiast who cannot cope with seeing Arthur C. Clarke's name being taken in vain, it may mean that you will not write a very good academic dissertation on the topic. On the other hand, avoid the risk of playing safe by returning to a text or author that you worked on during your pre-university studies because you feel secure and knowledgeable about it: in all probability, that is a misguided feeling. Use the dissertation as an opportunity to extend yourself. If you found reading Alice Walker's *The Color Purple* fascinating in a course on African-American Women's Writing, but want to read more by Walker and other African-American women writers, then use the dissertation as an opportunity.

In formulating a topic, you may be required to negotiate the genre of the proposal that is designed to map out the areas that you intend to cover when researching your topic. In common with most forms of academic writing, the dissertation proposal is an exercise that is at its best when it observes brevity and concision. Some programmes will provide their students with proformas that specify or advise a word limit for the proposal. They may also require you to provide an initial bibliographical account of the reading – primary and secondary – that your dissertation will take as a starting point. Even where such a proforma is not provided, it is not a bad idea to imagine such a structure for helping you to write the proposal. Your proposal should be based on the initial reading that you have completed; at the very least, it should cite texts that you know to be available and relevant. In your account of the intended thesis or motivating idea of the dissertation, indicate tendencies or a theme that interests you in your primary reading – for instance, the figure of the father in the poetry of Sylvia Plath – and then provide some indication or summary of the way in which this has been discussed in critical writing on Plath. Clearly this is not an original idea; but while originality is welcome, there is no expectation of an undergraduate dissertation that it needs to be original. Though you don't have to be original, your job is to engage inquisitively and searchingly with the poetry and the critical writing so that you can add an individual perspective to an already established topic. Your proposal can indicate how you might achieve this in the intended structure of your dissertation: you might begin with a chapter that establishes Plath's biography, her career as a writer of poetry and critical reactions to her poetry. In subsequent chapters, you might indicate how certain critical perspectives – for instance, psychoanalytic criticism and feminist literary theory – construct frameworks for discussing fathers and patriarchy, and how these can be brought to bear on a close reading of Plath's poetry. The aim in the proposal is not to write the dissertation or to state its conclusions. Instead, you are looking to convince your supervisor that you have devised a workable framework for undertaking a task that is realistic and achievable within word limits (if you have an 8,000-word dissertation, give up on the idea of writing about 'The Hero in Western Literature Since Homer').

Generally, you will be assigned to a supervisor who will guide you in writing the dissertation. Your supervisor may even help you with the proposal and to arrive at a workable title (use your experience of reading and interpreting essay questions to help you devise a title). Different institutions and programmes will issue different guidelines on access to supervision. In some places, you will be able to see your supervisor every week, in allotted time slots. In others, however, you may only be granted one or two initial meetings with your supervisor. Whatever the arrangements, it is important to remember that the dissertation is above all an independent piece of work. Your supervisor may be able to advise you on additional reading that you should consult (for example, a new article on Shakespeare that has just appeared). Your supervisor may even be able to comment on draft chapters that you have produced towards the final dissertation ('consider reworking this paragraph; what are you trying to say here?'). But do not mistake this for your supervisor 'telling you what to do'. In the end, you are responsible for the final product. Your supervisor will want the best for you, and will be keen for you to get a good grade. He or she will provide you with subtle hints and prompts to help you to improve the work. But in the end, a dissertation is a form of assessment that tests the extent of your critical reading, problem solving and writing skills.

10 RESEARCH AND WRITING SKILLS

10.1 RESEARCH SKILLS; OR, HOW TO PREPARE FOR ASSIGNMENTS

10.1.1 How to use the library

We have already mentioned the possible uses of your university's library and information services in Chapter 5 on reading. Your faculty or university library will be a likely port-of-call for secondary or contextual material when you are preparing for a teaching session – be it for a tutorial, workshop or seminar, or, perhaps, linked reading for a lecture. The library will also be a crucial resource when you have a major assignment or piece of assessment to complete, such as an essay, a dissertation, or a literature review.

Occasionally you may also borrow primary material from this source as well, though it should be stressed that on the whole you will be expected to purchase primary set texts for courses so that you have your own copy to refer to and speak from in teaching sessions. No university library can afford to offer individual copies of each set text for loan for all students; courses and modules will on the whole have been carefully costed to ensure that the purchase of primary texts and anthologies by individual students is economically viable. Often there will be a university bookshop – either on campus if you are at a campus-style university or otherwise at a designated site in your institution's local town or city – where copies of the set texts have been ordered in the numbers required for those taking the course.

When you are thinking about how to conduct or carry out contextual reading or preparatory work for an essay, course or module, reading lists will frequently provide an essential source of information. In addition, books you might take out on loan as a result of consulting these reading lists will contain their own useful bibliographies and suggestions for further reading. References in secondary texts of criticism are an invaluable means of extending and expanding your reading and thinking. In charting your own approaches to questions and assignments, it is a good idea to dip into and explore these alternative sites of information. Bear in mind that this is one obvious way in which you can indicate to a tutor, marker or assessor that you have adopted an individual approach to the task in hand, supplementing core course reading with your own reading paths. This invariably produces more original and individually inflected work than simply sticking to the recommended texts in mechanistic fashion. In a humanities subject like English, and especially in research-based assessment elements such as dissertations, individual thinking and independent research will be reflected in the marks and scores you are awarded. This independence factor will distinguish your project from those of other students as well as evidencing your commitment to scholarship. Not least, it will be proof of your ability to show initiative, which is a skill many employers enquire about on reference forms. No humanities course is interested in producing student automata that write identical answers to essay questions using the same narrow band of set texts or articles. The subject of English, as we have seen, is all about finding a personal path through disciplinary structures, one that reflects your own critical interests, personality and style.

As well as consulting books or taking them out on loan, it is helpful to remember the rich seam of ideas that can be found in the journals and periodicals section of the library. Some good reasons for accessing this particular resource have already been mentioned in Chapter 5 (pp. 73–4), and the same value of 'reading in layers' described there is relevant for the research methods being described here. In preparing for an essay question or answer, articles on the exact topic or theme of the question may not necessarily be available, but interesting and stimulating angles and approaches can often be suggested by careful reading around of a subject in journal articles and essays. Many journals are discipline-specific and sometimes focus on a particular period – for example, *English Literary Renaissance* or *Romanticisms* – and so can be especially helpful for sourcing historical or contextual material. Others are genre-based – such as *Screen* or *Theatre Journal* – or more generalised in their focus on the discipline, such as *Modern Language Review* or *Textual Practice*. Remember that multi-disciplinary or cross-disciplinary journals can also shed light on areas or approaches relevant to your purposes; examples of such journals include *Representations*, which looks at literary and visual arts across cultures and disciplines, or *Ecumene*, which has a focus on cultural geography.

Another important set of texts in the university library can be found in the reference section. Here you will encounter multi-volume collections such as encyclopedias, concordances and dictionaries. Some of these are especially helpful for English students. The *Oxford English Dictionary* will, for example, provide you with not only the multiple definitions of a particular word or phrase but also the etymologies of the same: the history of the word, how and when it was first used, and how its meanings have evolved over time into its present-day usage or usages. It might for example be helpful to know that when Ben Jonson or Charles Dickens used particular words they were coining them for the first time (such words are called neologisms) or that a word like 'licorish' meant something very different in an eighteenth-century novel to the confectionary-associated term we have today. The *OED-online* is also available in many universities so that you can carry out these searches and researches on a computer rather than in book-based form in the library.

Other texts that might be helpful include the *Dictionary of National Biography*, which will provide you with dates, overviews and publishing histories for particular writers and individuals relevant to your subject, and concordances which will give you a detailed record of the multiple uses of particular words in one author's canon of work. Concordances to Shakespeare are a particularly useful tool on English courses.

You can look up a word like 'remuneration' and be given every Shakespeare play and poem in which the term occurs as well as the precise act, scene or line reference. Equally helpful might be dictionaries of proverbs and commonplaces, or mythological or biblical tales. Many English students also find frequent reason to consult dictionaries of literary terms, so that they can pin down the precise meanings of terms like pastoral, epic or gothic. For some guidance on this, see the list of 'Further reading' at the back of this book.

University libraries are also storehouses of newspaper archives and more institution-specific material such as past examinations papers. Often they are also the site of film- and video-based work, which may be of especial interest if you are working on a film- or theatre-based module. They also provide practical assistance in the form of photocopying machines. The help desk and leaflets of advice will help you to make the best use of all of these provisions. Libraries are also information service providers in a more general sense. Computer terminals available there will enable you to consult or carry out research on specific CD-Rom-based material (there are, for example, several useful ones available on canonical literary figures such as Shakespeare, Dickens and George Eliot). These computers will also give you access to the Internet. All universities will have their own homepages and departmental websites may well be a useful source of information on staff, procedures and even specifics such as exam dates and reading lists. The following section will indicate ways in which the Internet can be used as a resource by literature undergraduates.

10.1.2 Selected Internet resources

In recent years, the Internet has become an essential research tool for undergraduates. Specific search engines and databases can be very helpful for English students. It would be impossible to provide a comprehensive account of the variety of research resources that are available to literature students. It is also unwise to even attempt to do so, in part because the services will probably have been modified by the time that this book has made it into print. Despite this, it will be helpful to provide some sense of the possibilities of two of the most established, academically authoritative and regularly used literature databases on the web.

A good starting point would be the MLA (Modern Languages Association of America) Bibliography, which can be accessed from First Search, a database that collects together a wide variety of bibliographical resources. The MLA Bibliography, regularly updated, is probably the most valuable resource for literature students in that it provides comprehensive information on journal articles, chapters in edited collections of books and completed Ph.D. theses listed in Dissertation Abstracts International. The MLA Bibliography works on the principle that these are the most difficult materials to identify and trace when doing research. We have indicated a way in which MLA might be consulted in Chapter 5 on Reading. Let's assume for a moment that you are searching for relevant journal articles or chapters from books in connection with an essay or dissertation topic on either Rushdie's *Midnight's Children*, or women in postcolonial writing. The MLA search engine is easy to use. It can be as uncomplicated as inserting the title of the work that you wish to research into the first 'keyword' field: a search on Rushdie's *Midnight's Children* has just yielded 137 essays to follow up. Clearly, this may be bordering on information overload, so it is important to remember that the search engine allows you to refine your searches. More than one field is available for 'keyword' searches. Thus, you may wish to insert 'postcolonialism' and 'women' in separate fields in order to look for material on the topic of women in postcolonial writing. You can limit the search to journal articles and writings in English (a search that yielded 29 articles). If you are accessing First Search/MLA through your library and information service (as you are most likely to), the search engine can even restrict the search to holdings available from your library. But this may be counter-productive if your library does not hold anything that the database might otherwise select: do not forget the importance of inter-library loans. And do not forget either that it may be possible to access journals that your library does not take in hard-copy format through JSTOR, an ever-expanding service that provides back runs of journals on line. However, at the time of writing its literature provision is not as strong as its provision for some other disciplines.

Another valuable web-based resource is Chadwyck-Healy's Literature On-line, or LION. This provides access to nearly three hundred and fifty thousand works on English and American literature, and related critical material. Specific browsing functions allow you to access brief biographies and bibliographies of literary figures (ranging from John Milton to Muriel Spark), and bibliographical references to criticism associated with specific authors and texts. A fair proportion of this criticism – indicated by a specific icon next to the bibliographical reference – is available in full-text version (though, remember, all of this material is copyrighted). Yet another browsing function gives you access to specially prepared study-guides to selected authors and texts, such as Achebe's novel *Things Fall Apart*. A very useful searching function enables you to scan for particular words and phrases in the literary works that are contained in the massive hypertext resources of the database. You may, for instance, want to know where the phrase 'great expectations' actually occurs in Dickens's novel of that name. Or, you may want to know where precisely Wordsworth articulates his 'spots of time' idea in the *Prelude*. The database will give you the reference, but will also take you, via a hypertext link, to the full extract of text in which the specific citation can be found. The website provides a facility for comments and suggestions to be fed back to the site's web master.

As already mentioned, there are now a number of on-line versions of the standard reference texts mentioned above, such as the *OED-online*, and it is likely that your university will subscribe to many of these. There are also web-specific databases on poetry, early modern texts and many other subjects that it will serve you well to familiarise yourself with. Many departmental websites will offer links to such sites. Some journals are also now published on line (such as *Renaissance Forum* and *Early Modern Literary Studies*). In addition linked websites on specific topics such as recent film releases or plays can provide useful and salient aids to study. However, we should also stress that the Internet comes with an Academic Health Warning in the small print! Not all sites or routes of information have been as rigorously checked or assessed as each other. Unlike most books and journals, which have gone through careful processes of scrutiny and sub-editing, a large number of websites contain biased or even inaccurate information. Part of the learning curve for any university student these days is therefore to acquire the skill of determining which material is worth accessing and how best to use it. In the case of on line journals or reference databases such as the *OED*, the reader can rest assured that the material is as valid as that to be found in the printed versions of the same. But on websites produced by groups with a particular position on the subject material – for example, a film production company advertising their own recent release or a pro-monarchy group's account of the execution of Charles I in 1649 – you would be well advised to test their claims against other more neutral sites or sources. It is best to develop a sense of judgement and discretion when dealing with material on the world wide web. Think about the nature of each individual site, how the information has been placed there and by whom, and what particular audience (if any) it is aimed at. A good example of how to exercise this kind of judgement and discretion is to think about college or personal websites where students may have posted versions of their own assignments. While it might be valid to consult some of these for models and ideas, bear in mind that you do not know how the work was assessed in many instances and the work may be more misleading than helpful. Also be aware that it is intellectually dishonest to download this work into your own essays unacknowledged. Due care and concern with this kind of material, which is becoming increasingly available, will help avoid unnecessary charges of plagiarism (for full details on this, see the relevant section on pp. 115–16). Many sites are now fully-fledged businesses, charging students for the dubious privilege of consulting or downloading other students' past essays. Not only is this a costly exercise, you are spending inordinate amounts of time looking at someone else's 'answers' instead of using that time to exercise your own thought. If studying English literature really is about finding your own voice, as we have tried to indicate throughout this volume, copying the work of others is simply denying yourself the full benefit of your degree studies. Have confidence in your own work and save your money for a good novel or a night at the cinema.

Despite some claims to the contrary, copyright does exist on the net and full acknowledgement needs to be given of sites used and you need to carefully check copyright laws on any visual or image-based material you wish to incorporate in your own projects. The best advice would be to read the Internet with a critical, honest and alert imagination.

10.1.3 Referencing research materials

Of course, as well as carrying out all this research for a particular assignment, you will also need to develop the skill of referencing your research accurately in essays and dissertations. This will usually occur in the shape of providing a bibliography at the back of assessed work as well as specific references – either in parentheses after the relevant quotation or allusion, or in footnote or endnote form – within the body of the essay, review or dissertation. References and bibliographies are important documentary records of your research methods and therefore any bibliography should indicate all the material you have consulted, including websites (see the previous section). Do not be tempted to add on lots of extraneous material you have not consulted to make your bibliography look longer since this documentation will often be used as a template for discussion should your work require a viva voce examination. A 'viva', as it is most commonly called, is an oral examination, usually conducted in the case of unresolved borderline degree classifications or in specific cases where a student was seriously ill for a particular assignment. The questions tend therefore to focus on a specific course or assignment. The examiners judge and assess what the standard of the student's work is from the viva. If you have claimed in a bibliography to be more widely read on a subject area than you are, it could lose you marks if you are asked questions about something you have not really read or consulted. As ever, honesty is always the best policy.

Bibliographies require the standardised provision of information on your reading and research. If you are including a book, for example, you will need to cite the author or editor's full name, the full title of the book, usually underlined or in italics, plus the publishing history of the text; that is, its place of publication – for example, Edinburgh – and the publisher – for example, Edinburgh University Press – as well as the year of publication. The order in which this information is placed does depend on the individual referencing system recommended by your institution or department (there are several frequently used versions). Your departmental or student handbook will usually make clear the preferred system – if not, consult your tutor or lecturer for further advice. The bibliography citation for this book might for example be set out thus:

David Amigoni and Julie Sanders, *Get Set for English Literature* (Edinburgh: Edinburgh University Press, 2003).

Or thus:

Amigoni, David and Julie Sanders (2003), *Get Set for English Literature* (Edinburgh: Edinburgh University Press).

If you have looked at specific chapters, essays, or articles in books you will also need to provide in your citation the full details of the author of the individual section, the title of the article (this time in single or double quote marks, depending on the system, not italicised or underlined) and the relevant page numbers on which the article or section occurs in the book. If you have looked at an article in a journal you require the author plus title (in quote marks) plus the title of the journal or periodical (in italics or underlined), the relevant volume number, the year of publication and the page numbers. If you have consulted websites you need the authors and titles of the pieces where available and the full website address. You need to list all of this information in alphabetical order. An example of what a bibliography might look like can be found in the 'Further reading' section of this publication. Provision of this information and documentation in full, and clear referencing throughout your written work of secondary and primary texts you have deployed, will avoid any of the problems surrounding plagiarism which are discussed on pages 115–16.

It is much easier to compile a bibliography if you have recorded all the necessary information each time you read and make notes on a book, article, review or website. In your note-taking, make sure you get into the habit of recording all the required information at the top of the page before you do anything else in relation to the text. Remember as you go along to record the precise page number where quotations or ideas are taken from so that you can reproduce this in an essay should you choose to use this work to inform your own – you might find it most helpful to put the individual page number in the margin each time you read and make notes from a new page so you know exactly where to go back to in the text should you wish to reconsult and so that your marker or tutor also has that information immediately to hand. It is all a simple matter of best practice and practice makes perfect in this instance as in so many others. Enter all the details on each text you have consulted in alphabetical order on a named computer file (call it 'Bibliography' and identify which essay or assignment it relates to – remember to back up the file regularly so the information cannot be lost) or by hand on an index-card filing system. This will make it much less arduous when compiling the final bibliography ready for submission.

As already mentioned, referencing systems are varied and different departments, schools or faculties will have different rules and requirements. Remember to consult the relevant handbook or website. If you are a dual or joint honours student you may have the added complication that different subjects reference differently: social sciences bibliographies tend to look rather different to humanities ones, for example. Some of the more common systems include the MHRA, the Chicago Style and the Harvard system (also referred to as the author-date system). University libraries often carry easily consultable reference books on these styles and in feedback sessions tutors will suggest ways to perfect your system of referencing. Don't panic: no one will expect you to be pitch-perfect the first time you do a bibliography. It is important that you try your best and learn where corrections need to be made. Referencing skills are something you acquire and they will come in handy in any job where filing or archival skills are recommended. Keeping an accurate personal filing system, be it on computer or paper, can really make life easy. As already stressed, no one will expect a first-year undergraduate essay to be perfect in all respects, but by the time you reach a final-year dissertation, accurate presentation and adherence to style guidelines may well be reflected in the marks awarded.

10.1.4 Choosing an essay question or dissertation topic, and establishing a plan

It is all very well understanding the methods of research but it is also important to think about how to select essay topics. As with the advice given in Chapter 9 on assessment (pp. 100–1), playing safe is not always the best option for any student. While it may seem a good idea to choose a topic that you've 'done before' in some form, perhaps in an A level or Highers context, this may not encourage you to stretch yourself and to apply newly-acquired skills of close reading and theoretical application. What might on the surface appear to be a 'hard' topic because it is unfamiliar may be just what you need to stretch your intellectual skills and capabilities to the utmost and may well result in a more ambitious and individual piece of writing. As with examination-type questions (which we discuss more in Chapter 11), you must take care to ensure you fully understand the essay question you have selected to answer. You can always double-check this by discussing it with a tutor; perhaps by taking them an essay plan to glance at. And, as with exam questions, make sure you stick to the task in hand: don't refashion questions to give the answer on a topic you wanted to come up as a choice. Digressions will not help you get the grades you want either: identify the essay's main questions and concerns and plan your essay to answer these in a coherent and logical and well-supported manner.

Essay plans are a really good habit to get into. Some students opt for highly detailed plans that set out the essay's aims and objectives in the form of a brief account of what each paragraph will discuss and cover and an outline of the introduction and conclusion. Others work with diagrammatic accounts of the structure and direction of an essay to ensure that diversions are not taken and problematic digressions made. Planning will indicate where secondary material or essential elements such as close reading and direct quotation should best be placed in an essay. Writing a plan, and possibly discussing it with a tutor, should therefore be considered an essential part of the research and preparation for writing an essay or dissertation and should not be hurried. On some modules you may even find its importance is recognised to the extent that submission of a plan may be compulsory and may even form part of the assessment marks.

Think about word lengths too. Word limits are established for writing assignments for good pedagogical reasons, not just so tutors can be punitive towards students who exceed or fail to reach them. There is genuine skill and acumen involved in writing concisely and coherently, so if your essay is over or under length, then make efforts to rectify the situation. If it is too long, consider ways to cut and edit that will tighten up the argument and make the work stronger overall. If it is too short, consider whether specific points need expansion or more support through quotation or secondary allusions. But always ask the question whether the material you are including is salient to the topic. Although sometimes the temptation is to pack in and display all the knowledge you have on a particular text or writer, this does not always serve the argument of an essay well. The power of selection is a crucial part of the range of intellectual strategies and techniques you develop on an English degree. Allowing yourself a reasonable amount of time to revise and rethink work in this way is therefore essential (for more detailed discussion of this point, see Chapter 8 on time management). A good general rule with essays then is to be bold, but stick to the point, plan well and observe the rules.

10.1.5 Plagiarism

Plagiarism occurs when, in an essay or any piece of assessed work, one takes and uses another's words, writings or ideas, and passes them off as one's own independent work. It is an academic crime in any discipline or subject area, and all universities and colleges will have in place quite rigorous, and often punitive, procedures for dealing with the problem when it is discovered. English literature is a discipline that is centrally concerned with responding to words written by others in a language that, while shaped and critically disciplined, is valued because it is your own. Because of this, teachers of English literature in higher education can, publicly at least, adopt a particularly intolerant attitude to the problem.

Lecturers will be justifiably intolerant of conscious and cynical plagiarism. This might occur, for example, when a student pays to download a completed essay from an Internet site designed for such a purpose, and hands it in as his or her own original work. Our advice here can scarcely be addressed to students who make the decision to play the system in this way: they are operating in a moral universe that we find difficult to recognise. However, it is our conviction that the majority of instances of plagiarism that do occur, and are discovered, are of a different order. Plagiarism can come about unconsciously because of incompetent or haphazard note-taking techniques. You may think that the words you are transcribing into your essay from your notes are words formulated by yourself when you read Elaine Showalter's essay on gender in *The Mayor of Casterbridge*. However, the marker of your essay will recognise them as Showalter's words that you have failed to quote accurately and honestly; even though there was no intention to deceive, and you have cited her essay in your bibliography. This is why it is very important to take careful and accurate notes that carefully differentiate between the words of a critic and your own commentary. Tutors will probably be more tolerant of this kind of unconscious plagiarism, especially at the beginning of your undergraduate career. However, if it is ever pointed out to you, you should be very careful not to repeat the error.

Plagiarism can also be a symptom of a crisis of confidence. We have said above that English literature values the voices of others transcribed in writing, and encourages its students to write about these writings in a voice of their own which is at once insightful and critically disciplined. Yet this is a genuinely hard thing to achieve. And what happens if you struggle to find your own voice, a fact evinced by your tutor's comment that your writing lacks coherence and fluency? It can be very tempting, on receiving this sort of feedback, to turn to a discourse which is fluent and authoritative, and simply to import the writing of a critic, unfiltered, into your essay. You should of course resist this temptation. It will introduce a jarring shift of register into your work, and your tutor will be able to spot this kind of plagiarism instantly. Nonetheless, work productively on the fact that you can identify effective academic writing. Attempt to imitate its moves and tones without copying it unthinkingly. And seek advice from your tutor about how to write more effectively.

10.2 WRITING SKILLS

The choice of topic, attendant research, planning and attention to matters of presentation and length are all part of the research skills involved in writing an essay or dissertation at university. But now we need also to think about the precise writing and compositional skills required by any such exercise or assignment. As ever, different forms of practice and methodology will suit different students. Some people prefer to write on paper first (this is sometimes referred to as longhand) and then to transfer that work on to a computer file. Others work straight on to the screen. Some write in note form first and then go back and 'fill in' the detail. Others write more methodically, paragraph by paragraph. There is no right or wrong in all of this, but there are elements of best practice that can be observed or encouraged and that is the thinking behind this section of the book.

Having selected your essay question or topic, bearing all the points made in the previous section about not 'playing safe' in mind, you should then 'brainstorm' your specific topic. Read and reread the primary text or texts, making question-specific notes as you go along. Make detailed notes on the theme or topic, the texts that will be relevant to your answer and possible passages you will focus on in any close reading. Doing this should also alert you to specific areas where secondary or contextual reading will prove especially helpful. Then look at this secondary material, making similarly detailed notes (and remembering to record all the details necessary for the purposes of the bibliography). Pinpoint material or ideas that will be salient to your discussion and that you will include in the final essay.

Now you can begin to assemble the detailed plan, structure or essay framework, that was mentioned as a crucial part of preparation for writing in the previous section (p. 114). Think about how you wish to argue your case and the order in which specific points or observations should emerge. Think too about the component parts of any essay – the introduction, the central points (often made in units of thought or expression referred to as paragraphs), and, of course, your summing up or conclusion. Once you have settled on your framework or plan, and made all the notes necessary from both primary and secondary material, you can start to write. If you have consulted a tutor or seminar leader about the plan, you may have made modifications and improvements to it by this stage.

Be prepared to draft and redraft the essay proper as well as the plan. Once again, time management will be key to this process (see Chapter 8). You may prefer to write in sections or to write the essay in its entirety and then redraft and rework. Different methods are all valid, provided they allow time for revision and improvement. It is not a good idea to only think about the whole assignment 48 hours before the due date and then try and write the whole thing in a splurge of coffee and stress the night before submission. Not only will you find most of the secondary material you might need is on loan already from the library and that your computer, sensing your stress, will choose this exact moment to crash but undoubtedly unnecessary errors will creep into your work. Allow time to rethink what you have written with a clear head and not only to proofread accurately, checking for errors of spelling and presentation, but also to re-evaluate and refine your arguments. Academic writing can only benefit from this kind of careful rethink. You can edit overlong essays for clarity and concision as recommended in the previous section's discussion of word length (pp. 114–15); you will also pick up on repetitions or contradictions in your work at this stage. This 'rethink' time also allows for attention to be paid to matters of tone and expression – if you are overusing one particular word or phrase you can revise the essay to read with greater variety and interest. All of these considerations will lead to a far more honed and engaging piece of writing, which will no doubt be reflected in the grade or mark awarded.

It is often the case that the clear sense of direction you had when you set out on the essay-writing path has actually undergone its own revisions and nuancing in the process and this may make it advisable to revise substantially any draft introduction you may have written. Some students actually find it easiest to leave the writing of the introduction until last because you don't always know exactly where you are going until you get there.

Equally important is to identify and be aware of what skills are required to write a good essay or dissertation. Clarity of argument is essential – this requires careful ordering and arrangement of your ideas so that points emerge sequentially and in relation to one another, rather than as a series of random observations. A good essay also comes down to the level of writing, pure and simple. You should make your case in good, clear sentences, attending to matters of syntax and phraseology. Paragraphs should lead into one another, bridging the argument as it is sometimes referred to, rather than standing as entirely discrete blocks that would render the essay a rather stilted read. You want to aim for flow and fluidity in the progress and development of the argument. See the 'Further reading' section for some books that go into these writing skills and how to develop and refine them in more detail.

The cogency and persuasiveness of your argument should also be a matter for concern when writing your essay. How are you developing the research you carried out? Quotations from both primary and secondary texts, as well as being accurately referenced, should do obvious work for you in the context of the essay and its argument. They should not resemble glittering jewels dropped in for display and effect but be an integral part of the point or points you are making. When you quote from a writer, novelist, dramatist, poet, or critic, you should always follow this up with a point or analysis, a response of some sort. This may entail close reading primary quotations, looking at how aspects such as metre, syntax or stress serve to further the argument, or agreeing with or refuting a critical observation. If you refute a point in this way, you must then offer evidential support for the reading or counter-observation you are making. Remember above all that an essay is your individual piece of work – secondary material is there to support your argument, and to offer deeper context or a voice to argue with: it should not drown out your individual responses entirely. Writing an essay is as much about the development of your critical voice as seminar discussions or group presentations.

It is advantageous to recall that literature essays often require that the student achieve a balance between close reading and wider contextual discussion. When structuring an essay, consider whether you have achieved that balance or what can be done to redress any imbalance such as weighting towards too much close quotation and not enough wider argumentation or vice versa. When you have more than one text or author under discussion in a single essay or exercise, the most sophisticated approach is always to interweave discussion of all the texts or writers rather than discuss each in turn, which can make an essay read rather fragmentarily.

Once written, remember all the recommendations to check essays and proofread them carefully given earlier in this section on Writing Skills. Spellcheckers in word-processing packages are huge aids but they will not catch every error or typo especially when one real word has been accidentally substituted for another. 'Robinson Crusoe lived on a topical island' or 'His ant chose never to marry' are examples of sentences containing an obvious mistake that a spellchecker device will not notice. Most students find it easiest to check off-screen: printing, that is, a draft copy of the essay on paper and marking up mistakes in pencil or pen that can be rectified on screen before the final print run. Sometimes it may be helpful to read the essay aloud, since mistakes your eye does not always detect (especially if you've been looking at the same few pages for a number of hours) will emerge in reading the text aloud. You'll also get used to hearing naturally where pauses occur, where punctuation is or is not needed, and where sentences are overlong and need careful division.

Finally, remember that essays are always opportunities to stretch and expand your skills. If you are interested in widening your vocabulary, invest in a good dictionary and use that to look up alternatives to words that you overuse or that sound too simplistic in the context of your essay. This is not an instruction to be verbose for the sake of it, but English is all about exploring the rich possibilities of the language in its written form and this applies as much to your own compositions as those of Milton or Martin Amis. A thesaurus is a further means of widening your linguistic register and many word-processing packages offer versions of these. While sometimes a writer who uses lots of words that you do not immediately understand may seem alienating, why not see the positive in this and use your dictionary to explore these new words instead of dismissing them and closing your mind to the possibilities?

10.2.1 What makes a good essay?

While the skills detailed above may all seem reasonably tangible objectives when writing an essay, the question still arises about what it is that separates a really good essay from an average one. Tutors and lecturers are asked this question endlessly and many departments will provide marking and assessment criteria in handbooks or on websites, detailing the qualities they look for in a 2:1 or a 2:2 essay or exam or when awarding specific percentage marks – that is what makes the difference between a high 2:1 and a low 2:1. The answer is always a complex combination of things: good and thorough attention to the question or topic; careful, thoughtful research that is well documented and applied; a well-written piece of work that is well organised, arranged, and presented, and which elicits a skilful use of language and attention to an author's or text's use of the same. More sophisticated essays, as already mentioned, will interweave a series of texts under discussion, and those that exhibit the potential at least to receive top grades will be clear and engaging but also show marks of individuality and independent thinking, as well as evidence of careful attention in seminars and lectures.

Adopting the right tone and style is crucial to developing your writing skills. This is, as already stressed, not a case of using lots of long words for the sake of it. Verbosity does not necessarily equal articulate expression: it is always better to strive for clarity. But it is important to recall at all times that academic writing is a formal discourse and you should observe this in the idiom you adopt in the context of your essays. Here are some helpful pointers to achieving the correct tone:

1. Avoid slang or overly conversational styles. While it is admirable to have your own voice, being too idiosyncratic in this formal context can sometimes work against you in the assessment procedure. As ever, it is a matter of balance.
2. Try not to be outspoken without just cause.
3. You must always support points.
4. Develop a varied and lively vocabulary with the help of a good dictionary.
5. Try to avoid the repetition of the same phrase or word over and over again in the course of the same essay. (A sentence that is not very good will not be very good at varying what it has to say in the course of the sentence – see what we mean?)
6. Aim for the argument to flow easily and naturally. Engage your reader. Reading aloud for sense and meaning can be helpful here.
7. Vary sentence length. An essay composed of entirely short staccato sentences will not have much flow, but equally an essay composed only of long sentences could be a confusing read. Reading aloud for sense can be helpful here too.
8. Think carefully about the power and importance of the introduction and conclusion in the structure of an essay. Make sure yours packs a punch!
9. Think about the different discursive contexts of written and/or oral assignments. A presentation has different requirements to a long essay. A dissertation is completely different to a book review. Learning to identify contexts and the suitable languages and registers for each is another skill you will acquire gradually.

10. As with the authors you study, learn the conventions and then you can afford to be more ambitious with what you try to do within the essay or dissertation context. With the right foundations you can do anything, without them your essay will collapse.

Checklist
To recap, there are some simple rules, then, which we have already outlined that will help to secure good marks in an essay or exam answer. These would include:

1. Sticking to the question.
2. Detailed planning.
3. Careful and thorough presentation.
4. Proofreading and revision (this requires time management).
5. Accurate and thoughtful referencing.
6. A full and accurate bibliography.
7. Observing word limits.

More esoteric, but nonetheless crucial, points to bear in mind which will help to improve or sustain your grades would include:

1. Not playing safe when selecting the question.
2. Adopting the right tone and style.
3. Interweaving discussion of focus texts and authors.
4. Insightful and integral deployment of quotation.
5. Achieving a balance between close reading and wider discussion.
6. Original thinking.

10.2.2 Getting feedback on essays you have completed

It is all very well knowing the foundations of what makes a good essay but it is also crucial that you regard each assignment that you complete in the course of your university career as part of the learning curve as well as simply an exercise in achieving grades. Lecturers and tutors will invariably offer feedback sessions on completed assignments. These are the means by which you can identify your strengths and weaknesses as a critic and writer. You can learn from mistakes, identifying areas for attention, such as woolly use of punctuation or poor referencing. Tutors can identify areas of tone or register and how you might improve these formal aspects of your writing; they might also suggest ways to sharpen up structure or your use of quotation. Feedback sessions should be regarded as an integral part of your learning programme, as essential as any seminar or lecture. As well as pouring time and energy into researching and writing essays, do the follow up on what were the good points about what you have achieved and how you might expand on them in future. If there is one thing to learn as an undergraduate, it is to exploit all aspects of the systems and structures that are in place to help and guide your learning and personal development.

11 REVISING FOR AND TAKING EXAMINATIONS

Having struggled through A Level or Higher examinations, some students of English arrive in higher education with the hope that time-limited examinations in silent great halls are a thing of the past. This may be the case: some programmes do not use this method of assessment. However, if you have sought to consign examinations to the past then you need to be aware that many, if not the majority of, programmes do continue to use the examination as one method of assessment. Sad to say, but one reason for retaining examinations is increasingly a 'defensive' one. Plagiarism is now a major source of anxiety for tutors, and examinations are a very effective way of ensuring that students can write independently, in their own voices, about the literature that they have been studying. However, it is important to emphasise the fact that it is now just one method of assessment. Once upon a time, the dreaded notion of 'finals' loomed before all undergraduate students. That is to say, a series of examinations taken at the end of the final year which tested students on all the literary knowledge they had acquired over two or three years. Although the term 'finals' is still used, in most cases it no longer accurately reflects that former and rather scary sense of 'finality'. Generally speaking, an examination will now be one item of assessment on a module; it may accompany an essay and some other form of assessment (such as a class presentation). Consequently, it will probably be a weighted component of a total package of assessment, or 'worth' a percentage of the total marks available on the module. And you will take the exam at the end of the module, not necessarily at the end of your degree studies. Because examinations assess the knowledge and skills you have studied on the module, you will find it helpful to your revision to familiarise yourself with the stated aims, learning outcomes and 'assessment menu' of the module. For instance, one component of the exam may consist of an exercise in close reading, or the exam itself may test you on the material studied only in the latter weeks of the module.

11.1 DIFFERENT MODELS OF EXAMINING

Before saying more about revision and approaches to examinations, it may be helpful to note another consequence of tutors' having to assess on the basis of learning outcomes in modules. This way of thinking has had a productive effect on the variety of examination methods that are now available. Although the timed, sit-down examination remains the most common, you may also get the opportunity to take a seen examination or a takeaway paper, as these may be the most appropriate ways of assessing your grasp of particular kinds of knowledge and skills. For instance, a theory exam may expect a level of self-reflexivity that would best be served by your taking the examination paper away and completing it within a stipulated time-frame (say, overnight). Or, you may be studying a module concerned with the relation between literature and film, focusing particularly on the question of adaptation between novel and film. The examination may seek to assess your skill in comparing and contrasting scenes from novels and their filmic adaptations, focused around particular thematic questions. Of course, open-book examinations are increasingly to be found at both A Level and in higher education, but film presents quite distinct problems again. Because it would be impossible to have an examination hall full of video screens, the examination described is seeking learning outcomes that might best be served by a seen paper. This would allow you to prepare the questions you seek to answer in advance by working on relevant films and scenes from novels. While such exams may seem 'easier' than the conventional, memory-based kind, a brief word of caution: these exams give you the opportunity to prepare, and you ought to take full advantage of that opportunity, but you can overprepare through memorising by rote the precise answer that you intend to write out in the exam hall. The best exam answers are of course well informed and detailed, but they also have a degree of spontaneity about them whereby the marker can see thought taking place and shaping itself to the question. It may seem odd to say this but, aside from nerves, one of the main difficulties that students can experience in examinations is a curious loss of motivation and drive. Such a loss of motivation is more likely to happen as a result of thinking you know exactly what you will write out in the examination. To avoid boring yourself, and the marker who will read what you have written, do not shy away from placing yourself under the kind of pressure that will keep you productively focused on being creative under exam conditions.

One of the main misapprehensions about all examinations is that they are memory tests. The impulse to think in these terms about literature exams can be strong. For many students their first memories of poetry involve learning it 'by heart'. It can be quite common for students to worry unduly about the need to remember quotations from poems, novels or plays (though less so as open-book examinations become more common). Rote learning and repetition do not actually tell an examiner very much about the literary knowledge that someone can use. But this begs the question: how should one revise to pass a literature exam, and what is being assessed? It needs to be recognised that, first, there is no universal model of successful revision. And, second, that literature is a difficult kind of knowledge to consolidate. You may know the dates of Angela Carter's life, but this will not help you to answer a question on the importance of the idea of the carnivalesque to *Nights at the Circus*. There is a sense in which revision can be comfortingly dull and dutiful: if you sit there for long enough with a set of notes before your passive and glazed eyes, then you can convince yourself that something useful is 'going in'. You need to remember that a literature exam is assessing you on discussion-based approaches to texts; that is to say, reading texts in relation to critical and cultural contexts, and the construction of arguments. Consequently, it is above all important to take an active approach to revision. What follows are suggested active styles of, or approaches to, revision, remembering all the while the object of assessment.

11.2 METHODS OF REVISION

Rereading is a good method of revision, though to be effective, it does need to be rereading and not a first acquaintance with the material concerned. Rereading can, however, be as passively ineffective as gazing at notes, only in this instance it is the authority of the primary text that is a source of comfort. Rereading is most effective when it is done in conjunction with the lecture notes and detailed analytical notes that you have taken in support of your own initial preparation for seminar or class discussions. Rereading can help you to 'repossess' the text in preparation for the exam: that is to say, a fresh reading of the text can help you to acquire the level of detail that is important for writing convincing and confident examination answers.

An excess of detail can, however, turn into a problem. Exam answers that indiscriminately list detail upon detail can be as problematic as exam answers that demonstrate a less than secure knowledge of the text. For revision purposes, you need to find ways of organising your detailed knowledge into potential arguments. Past examination papers can be a useful revision tool here (universities normally archive these documents in their libraries). The intelligent use of past examination papers needs to be distinguished from the rather less secure method of 'question spotting', which is a kind of racecourse-form approach to examinations. Rather than trying to convince yourself that it's two to one on that a question on magic realism in *Midnight's Children* will come up this year, acquaint yourself with the generic forms of questions that have been posed on Rushdie's narrative techniques and their sources. Besides 'magic realism' these might include questions on 'postmodernism', or 'historiographic metafiction'. Often such questions are framed by quotations from named critics (such as Linda Hutcheon, who coined the idea of 'historio-graphic metafiction'). Use these quotations constructively; they can direct you to the work of critics who will return you to the original or representative forms of critical argument in which texts have been discussed. As ever, approach sec-ondary materials in an active and analytical way. Don't simply 'raid' articles and books for usable ideas: you can end up with a completely contradictory *pot-pourri* of critical views. In-stead, try to understand the critical orientation and rationale of what you are reading; compare and contrast approaches to 'magic realism' and 'postmodernism'. Ask yourself which cultural contexts or aesthetic issues have been most success-fully elucidated by these terms. Ultimately, a successful exam answer is based upon a coherent argument, so you need to be sure about the terms in which you will ground your argument as well as the terms of the argument on which you are being invited to comment.

11.3 THE BIG DAY: TAKING THE EXAM

It remains to say something about actually taking the exam-ination and producing this coherently argued and informed script. Again, there are no universal solutions to this. If writing your answers while compulsively eating a bag of barley-sugar sweets and hugging a Pooh-bear-shaped hot-water bottle has always worked for you in the past, then why break a winning formula? However, idiosyncratic preferences aside, there are certain common factors that must determine your approach to the exam. The first and most obvious is that it is time limited, and that you must answer a set number of questions. This means that you need to time manage in a serious and self-disciplined manner. Diligent and well-prepared students can fail examinations because they have failed to manage the time of the examination properly. You need to remember that although that you can write a brilliant answer for section A, unless you answer on section B as well, you are quite likely to fail or at best scrape a pass (your one mark for section A will still be divided by two and averaged). You must, therefore, read and obey the rubric, or the words that direct your conduct in the examination (how many questions you must answer, and from which sections you must select). In time managing your examination, you also need to factor in a variety of activities aside from writing the answers. You should read the paper in as critical and analytical a manner as nerves and anxiety will allow. All too often, nerves, panic or perhaps complacency can lead you to mistake the question that has actually been asked for the question you were hoping would appear. To avoid writing an inadvertently irrelevant answer, you need to read closely the questions that you plan to tackle. Remember, you have been educated to a high level in the skill of reading! Often, breaking the question into its component parts can help here. In doing this, seek to work out the critical issue(s) that are embedded in the structure of the question (if you have been doing this in revision, it is much easier to do in the exam).

Always try to plan your argument in response to this question before you start to write; planning can help to keep your argument on the relevant track. In Chapter 10 we discussed the importance of writing essay plans prior to tackling major assignments. While the time-limited nature of an examination precludes any attempt at a detailed plan, rudimentary plans should still be sketched. These can grow out of your work on breaking down the terms of the question: having established what it is asking for, what is the best structure for answering this question, satisfying its terms. What are the details that you will use to illustrate and support your argument? Clearly, the bulk of your time will be best spent on realising your plan in prose. But planning in diagrams or brief notes for five or ten minutes can be time well spent. Not only will the plan keep you on track during your argument, but, in addition, if you do miscalculate timing, you have a plan in your examination book to which you can direct the examiner. Examiners, understandably, can really only award marks from the higher classifications to completed examination answers that comprise rounded and realised arguments.

However, it may be that your incomplete answer, taken in conjunction with your plan, will provide the examiner with enough of a sense of where your argument was going. Your overall performance on the paper, despite an incomplete answer, might be enhanced. Finally, let's end on a positive note. The exam has gone well for you, and you got the time management right. Still, you should remember the usefulness of allowing some time at the end of the examination to read through your script in order to eradicate unnecessary errors.

BIBLIOGRAPHY AND FURTHER READING

BIBLIOGRAPHICAL REFERENCES

Althusser, L. (1971), *Lenin and Philosophy, and Other Essays*, trans. Ben Brewster (London: NLB).

Brett, R. L. (1971), *S. T. Coleridge* (London: Bell).

Dickens, C. (1965), *Great Expectations*, Penguin English Library (Harmondsworth: Penguin).

Eagleton, T., and Milne, D. (eds) (1996), *Marxist Literary Theory* (Oxford: Blackwell).

Lodge, D. (ed.) (1972), *Twentieth-Century Literary Criticism: A Reader* (London: Longman).

Moran, J. (2002), *Interdisciplinarity*, New Critical Idiom (London: Routledge).

Richards, I. A. (ed.) (1977), *The Portable Coleridge*, Viking Portable Library (Harmondsworth: Penguin).

Roe, N. (1988), *Wordsworth and Coleridge: The Radical Years* (Oxford: Clarendon).

Said, E. (1978), *Orientalism* (London: Routledge).

Said, E. (1993), *Culture and Imperialism* (London: Chatto).

Wylie, I. (1988), *Young Coleridge and the Philosophers of Nature* (Oxford: Clarendon).

Young, R. J. C. (2001), *Postcolonialism: An Historical Introduction* (Oxford: Blackwell).

All references to Shakespeare are taken from the 1997 *Norton Shakespeare*, Stephen Greenblatt (gen. ed.) (London and New York: Norton).

FURTHER READING

1. Introductions to English Literature

Beard, A. (2001), *Texts and Contexts: Introducing Literature and Language Study* (London: Routledge).
Written by the Chief Examiner for AS/A Level English, this workbook establishes a helpful framework for reading the languages of literature in context, and sets well conceived exercises backed up by lucid commentaries. Its approach reflects the

changes that A Level literature is undergoing. Not as advanced as, for example, Hopkins 2001 (see below), the book could be either a helpful starting point for those new to literary study, or a useful refresher.

Eaglestone, R. (2000), *Doing English: A Guide for Literature Students* (London: Routledge).
A valuable and accessible book, it aims to bridge the gap between A Level and degree work in English. The book is particularly valuable for the way in which it introduces some of the major conceptual debates that have underpinned literary criticism and theory (such as authorial intention). It also explores the changes in literary studies in a chapter that is helpfully focused around the effects of these changes on Shakespeare studies.

Goring, P., Hawthorn, J., and Mitchell, D. (2001), *Studying Literature: The Essential Companion* (London: Arnold).
Part of the Arnold *Studying* series (other genre-specific volumes in the series are recommended under Section 3 below). This sizeable volume has preliminary sections on lectures, essay writing and practical aspects of studying literature as a discipline. There is also an extensive and extremely useful second section on the use of electronic media in the subject. Subsequent sections cover theories and approaches, literary terminology, and the final section offers a guide to specific theorists. Lists and selections such as the latter will always be subjective choices, but, nevertheless, this book provides useful groundings in many of the main areas of the subject that we have highlighted here.

Hopkins, C. (2001), *Thinking About Texts: An Introduction to English Studies* (Basingstoke: Palgrave).
An excellent guide to the development of reading skills for first-year English students. It contains a good and varied range of textual examples, and sophisticated yet accessible discussions of questions such as the nature of literature, the role of authors and critics, as well as the central interpretive questions that arise around genre, history and identities. If not formally adopted as a course textbook, it would make very helpful support reading for first-year students on any introductory course.

Jacobs, R. (2001), *A Beginner's Guide to Critical Reading: An Anthology of Literary Texts* (London: Routledge).
An interesting variation on the anthology, this presents texts ranging from the poetry of the sixteenth-century Thomas Wyatt to the late twentieth-century poetry of Elizabeth Bishop: prose and drama texts are well represented too. The texts are supplemented by interesting and thoughtful commentaries that are good illustrations of a subtle blend of literary critical and theoretical reading.

Klarer, M. (1999), *An Introduction to Literary Studies* (London: Routledge).
Originally published in German in 1998, this introduces the major literary genres, and central critical approaches; it also provides advice on secondary reading and essay writing. Contains a useful general introduction to the study of film in the context of literary studies.

Pope, R. (1998), *The English Studies Book* (London: Routledge).

Useful and extensive source for advice and information on the mechanics of analysing and studying literature.

Rylance, R., and Simons, J. (eds) (2001), *Literature in Context* (Basingstoke: Palgrave).
A helpful introduction with range of author-focused chapters by period specialists addressing the question of reading in 'context' from Chaucer to Toni Morrison. The editors and contributors are executive members of CCUE (Council for College and University English), and have collaborated with QCA (Qualification and Curriculum Authority) over the reform of AS/A Level nationally.

2. Literary history

Alexander, M. (2000), *A History of English Literature*, Macmillan Foundations (Basingstoke: Macmillan).
An introductory illustrated account of English literary history, from medieval literature to the present.

3. Literary criticism and theory

Lodge, D. (ed.) (1972), *Twentieth-Century Literary Criticism: A Reader* (London: Longman).
Valuable and durable collection of essays on major developments in literary criticism in the twentieth century; it includes essays by Abrams, Freud, Orwell, D. H. Lawrence, and a good selection of Anglo-American 'New Critical' writings.

Lodge, D. (ed.) (1988), *Modern Criticism and Theory* (London: Longman).
The 'follow up' and companion volume, so to speak, to Lodge 1972 (above). This volume provides a good range of the material that has been used to construct 'high' literary theory; it includes writings by de Saussure, Lacan, Derrida, Barthes, Kristeva, and Said.

Selden, R. (ed.) (1988), *The Theory of Criticism: From Plato to the Present* (London: Longman).
A remarkable anthology of extracts that mixes literary critical and theoretical writings from the earliest times to the present: the materials are organised around topics, such as representation, subjectivity, form and structure, history and society, and morality, class and gender.

Webster, R. (1996), *Studying Literary Theory: An Introduction* (London: Arnold).
An accessible introductory guide that explains traditional approaches in the light of the changes that theory has brought to bear on literature, as well as introducing some of the major themes and questions in the study of theory.

Wolfreys, J., and Baker, W. (eds) (1996), *Literary Theories: A Case Study in Critical Performance* (Basingstoke: Macmillan).

A series of chapters that takes a single text – a short story by Richard Jefferies – and performs different critical readings of that text from different theoretical perspectives (formalist, feminist, Marxist and deconstructionist).

New Accents: this series, under the general editorship of Terence Hawkes, published first by Methuen, and subsequently by Routledge, played a very important role in introducing theoretical ideas to mainstream literary studies from the late 1970s to the early 1990s. Influential titles include Terence Hawkes (1977), *Structuralism and Semiotics*; Tony Bennett (1979), *Formalism and Marxism*; Catherine Belsey (1980), *Critical Practice*; Christopher Norris (1982), *Deconstruction: Theory and Practice*. New and revised editions of some of the most influential works are now being re-issued by Routledge.

New Critical Idiom: this immensely valuable series, published by Routledge, offers students concise but considered introductions to many of the main terms and concepts they will encounter on a literature course. Titles such as Philip Hobsbaum (1996), *Metre, Rhythm, and Verse Form*, and Paul Cobley (2001), *Narrative*, deal with issues of form, while others deal with questions of genre such as Fred Botting (1996), *Gothic*, and Terry Gifford (1999), *Pastoral*. Central schools of literary theory are also explored in volumes such as Paul Hamilton (1996), *Historicism*, and Ania Loomba (1998), *Colonialism/Postcolonialism*. Recent publications in the series have also attempted to interrogate the discipline of literary study itself with titles such as Peter Widdowson (1999), *Literature*, Graham Allen (2000), *Intertextuality*, and Joe Moran (2002), *Interdisciplinarity*.

Also helpful for thinking about approaches to specific genres are the books published by Arnold under the following headings:

Hawthorn, J. (2001), *Studying the Novel*, 4th edn (London: Arnold).

Matterson, S., and Jones, D. (2000), *Studying Poetry* (London: Arnold).

Wallis, M., and Shepherd, S. (2002), *Studying Plays*, 2nd edn (London: Arnold).

4. Literary terms

Abrams, M. H. (1993), *A Glossary of Literary Terms* (Orlando: Holt).

The standard reference book for literary terms and phrases. A useful purchase for any English undergraduate.

Peck, J., and Coyle, M. (2002), *Literary Terms and Criticism*, 3rd edn (Basingstoke: Palgrave).

Organised by genre, this offers practical tips on carrying out analyses of literary texts as well as definitions of significant terms and phrases.

5. Study skills

Miller, L. (2001), *Mastering Practical Criticism* (Basingstoke: Palgrave).

Occasionally outmoded in its choice of terminology and its sense of expectation, there are nevertheless some very useful sections here on writing essays and preparing for examinations.

Myers, T. (2002), *Upgrade Your English Essay* (London: Arnold).
This is aimed at first-year undergraduates seeking to improve their grades in essays and examinations, and offers advice on structure, argumentation and modes of analysis in a down-to-earth style.

Peck, J., and Coyle, M. (1999), *The Student's Guide to Writing, Grammar, Punctuation, and Spelling* (Basingstoke: Macmillan).

Stott, R., Snaith, A., and Rylance, R. (eds) (2001), *Making Your Case: A Practical Guide to Essay Writing*, Speak-Write series (London: Longman).
The Speak-Write Project, organised from Anglia Polytechnic University, made an important contribution to thinking systematically about study skills in literature teaching. This volume addresses essay writing; it contains valuable advice about planning, writing and editing.

Other useful books in this series include:

Stott, R., and Avery, S. (2001), *Writing with Style* (London: Longman).

Stott, R., and Chapman, P. (2001), *Grammar and Writing* (London: Longman).

Stott, R., Young, T., and Bryan, C. (2002), *Speaking Your Mind: Oral Presentation and Seminar Skills* (London: Longman).

INDEX

A levels, 20–1
Althusser, Louis, 8, 52, 56–9
Atkinson, Kate
  Behind the Scenes at the Museum, 16
  Human Croquet, 15
assessment methods, 39–46, 95–102
Austen, Jane (*Sense and Sensibility*), 22–4

Barthes, Roland, 7, 52
Behn, Aphra (*Oronooko*), 26–7
bibliographical databases, 107–8
bibliographies, 111–13
book reviews, 44, 98–9

canon, 5
Carey, Peter (*Jack Maggs*), 17, 61–3
close reading
  as tool of assessment, 42–3
  drama, 13–14
  novel and prose narrative, 15
  poetry, 12–14, 69–70
Coe, Jonathan (*The Rotter's Club*), 15
Coleridge, S. T. ('Fears in Solitude'), 68–74
comparative literature, 5

concordances, 105–6
consultation, 34–6
context, 17
conventions, 12
course diaries, 42
courses (typical)
  literature and science, 48–9
  race and literature, 18
  Romanticism, 17

Dickens, Charles (*Great Expectations*), 17, 53–61
dictionaries, 120–1
  Dictionary of National Biography, 105
  literary terms, 106, 135
  Oxford English Dictionary, 105
dissertation, 35, 44, 99–102
  proposal, 101
  supervision, 102

Eliot, George (*Middlemarch*, *The Lifted Veil*), 48–9
English language, 19, 67
English literature
  and chronology, 47–8
  and colonialism, 8–9
  and 'communication age', 11
  and extra-mural activity, 19
  and quality, 49–50
  and questioning mind, 17
  as discipline/subject, 7–10

as writings in English, 4–5
in history, 3–4, 7
what it is, 3–10, 132–4
why study?, 11–20
essay(s), 40–1, 96–8, 121–3
  balance in, 120
  feedback on, 36–7, 123–4
  plans and drafts, 41, 114,
    117–19
  questions, 96–7, 113–14
  word limits, 114–15
examination(s), 45, 125–8
  feedback on, 36
  revision for, 128–9
  rubric, 130
  taking of, 129–30
  viva voce, 110–11

feedback, 36–8
feminism, 15, 60
Foucault, Michel, 8, 52

genre, 12
Graff, Gerald, 59

historicity, 50; *see also* New
  Historicism

iconography, 31
ideological state apparatuses,
  58
independent research, 38–9
interdisciplinarity, 9
internet, 106–10
intertextuality, 15
Ishiguro, Kazuo (*The Remains
  of the Day*), 16

journals, 73–4, 105
Joyce, James (*Ulysses*), 14–15

Lacan, Jacques, 56–7
learning and teaching
  situations, 20–39
  place of tutor's research in,
    39
Leavis, F. R., 5–6
lectures, 28–34
  examples of, 30–3
  getting the most from, 75–9
  note-taking in, 78
  relationship to seminars/
    tutorials, 86–7
  styles of delivery, 79
library, 67–8
  how to use, 103–6
literary criticism, 9–10, 55
literary history, 134
literary theory, 6–7, 17, 50–63,
  134–5
  aims, 50
  and cultural literacy, 63
  and literary criticism, 55
  and principled debate, 59–60
  approaches to, 52–3
  feminist, 60
  'high', 53–9
  'moment of', 52
  see also New Historicism,
    postcolonialism
literature reviews, 43
Luhrmann, Baz (*Romeo +Juliet*
  [film]), 27–8

Marxism (structuralist), 52–9;
  see also structuralist
  linguistics
'media age', 11
mesmerism, 62–3
modularity, 6, 47–50
Moran, Joe, 50–1
multidisciplinarity, 9

narrative, 15–17, 55
    and imperialism, 61
New Historicism, 62–3
note-taking
    in lectures, 78
    in seminars/tutorials, 88

Oates, Joyce Carol (*Black
    Water*, *Blonde*), 24–5
oral presentations, 45–6, 89,
    95–6
orientalism *see* postcolonialism;
    see also Said, Edward
Oxford English Dictionary,
    105

peer assessment, 46, 90
periodisation, 4
Petrarch, 12
plagiarism, 115–16
pleasure, 14; *see also* reading
politics, 15
postcolonialism, 60–2
postmodernism, 16
portfolios (writing and
    research), 42
progress reviews, 37–8
proofreading, 120

quotations, 119

readers, 58
reading, 55
    and time management, 93
    'in layers', 67–74
    lists, 103–4
    primary texts, 12–14, 68–70
    secondary texts, 71–4
referencing and citation, 73–4,
    97–8, 110–13
research skills, 103–15

Roe, Nicholas (*Wordsworth
    and Coleridge: the Radical
    Years*), 71–2
Romanticism, 8, 17

Said, Edward (*Orientalism*),
    60–1
Saussure, Ferdinand de, 56
seminar learning and teaching,
    21–5
    attendance at, 85–6
    discussion in, 87–8
    expectations at final year,
        24–5
    expectations at level one,
        22–4
    follow up on, 90–1
    how to use, 80–91
    note-taking in, 88
    oral presentations in, 89
    preparation for, 82–5
    relationship to lectures, 86–7
Shakespeare, William
    Hamlet, 13–14
    'Sonnet 20', 12–13
Sterne, Laurence (*Tristram
    Shandy*), 16
structuralist linguistics, 56–7
study skills, 11–19, 67–131,
    136
    and employability, 18–19
subjectivity, 8, 11
subject position, 57
supervision, 34–6
symbolic order, 57

time management, 92–4
tutorial learning and teaching
    see seminar learning and
    teaching

Warner, Marina (*Indigo*), 15
websites, 109–10
Williams, Raymond, 6
workshops, 25–8

expectations at final year,
    27–8
expectations at level one,
    25–6
writing skills, 117–21, 136